Aviation Elite Units

No 126 Wing
RCAF

2017

Aviation Elite Units • 35

OSPREY
PUBLISHING

No 126 Wing RCAF

Donald Nijboer
Series editor Tony Holmes

First published in Great Britain in 2010 by Osprey Publishing,
PO Box 883, Oxford, OX1 9PL, UK
PO Box 3985, New York, NY 10185-3985, USA
Email: info@ospreypublishing.com

Osprey Publishing is part of the Osprey Group.

Transferred to digital print on demand 2014.

First published 2010
1st impression 2010

Printed and bound by PrintOnDemand-Worldwide.com, Peterborough, UK.

A CIP catalogue record for this book is available from the British Library.

ISBN 13: 978 1 84603 483 1
PDF e-book ISBN: 978 1 849082624

Editorial by Tony Holmes
Page design by Mark Holt
Cover artwork by Mark Postlethwaite
Aircraft profiles and Unit Insignia by Chris Davey
Index by Alan Thatcher
Originated by PQD Digital Media Solutions, Suffolk, UK

www.ospreypublishing.com

Front Cover
By December 1944 the threat posed by the Me 262 jet fighter to 2nd Tactical Air Force airfields in Holland and Belgium was very different to that faced by American bomber crews attacking targets over Germany. Based at B88 Heesch, in Holland, No 126 Wing was operating from one of the most forward Allied bases in-theatre, close to the heavily defended Me 262 bases in western Germany. In No 126 Wing's area of operation Me 262s operated singly in the 'blitz bomber' role, and as soon as they saw a fighter they turned for home at high speed. The German fighter's shark-like tactics were effective, but caused very little material damage. Their ability to avoid early detection, approach RAF airfields with great speed, drop their bombs and quickly escape caused both shock and disbelief for those on the ground.

On 25 December 1944 Flt Lt John J Boyle of No 411 Sqn caught one such Me 262 while flying his Spitfire IXE MK686/DB-L. That morning No 126 Wing had been ordered into the air to provide maximum air support in the American sector during the 'Battle of the Bulge'. The fighters of No 411 Sqn were the last to take off, and on the way to their area of operation, Flt Lt Boyle's wingman developed a 'ropy' engine. Squadron protocol dictated that Boyle escort his No 2 back to base. He described what happened next;

'As we neared Heesch we were far too high, and in order to get rid of the excess height I stuck the nose almost straight down in a screaming spiral dive. As my speed shot past 500 mph, out of nowhere appeared an Me 262. It took only a second to see to my gunsight and safety catch, and then I was right behind him. My first burst of cannon fire hit his port engine pod, which began streaming dense smoke. He immediately dove for the deck as an evasive tactic, but with only one engine now working he couldn't outrun me. I scored several more hits before he clipped some tall treetops and then hit the ground at an almost flat angle. His aircraft disintegrated in stages from nose to tail as it ripped up the turf for several hundred yards until only the tail assembly was left.'

The Me 262 belonged to II./KG 51, and it was being flown by Oblt Hans-Georg Lamle. This was Boyle's second aerial victory, and he would 'make ace' on 14 January 1945. His score at war's end stood at five and one shared destroyed.

No 126 Wing destroyed or damaged more German jet fighters and bombers than any other unit in the 2nd TAF (*Cover artwork by Mark Postlethwaite*)

CONTENTS

INTRODUCTION

No 126 Wing was a mobile fighter-bomber wing – one of the greatest fighting machines in history. Formed in July 1943 as part of the Royal Air Force's 2nd Tactical Air Force (TAF), its mandate was to carry out air-to-air combat and ground attack sorties in direct support of the British and Canadian armies once they had landed on the continent. From D-Day to the end of the war, No 126 Wing was the most successful fighter outfit in the 2nd TAF, claiming an incredible 336 enemy aircraft destroyed. Different published sources put the grand total for the wing from its inception at between 355 and 365 aircraft destroyed.

Why was No 126 Wing so successful, and how did it rack up such an impressive score in what was essentially the last year of the war, and one in which the Luftwaffe was in rapid decline? To answer these questions we have to look at the genesis of Allied tactical air power, as well as its long gestation period.

At the start of World War 2 there were two very different ideas on how air power should be used in a future conflict. For its part the RAF focused on the new doctrine of strategic bombing, its founders and early leaders believing that destroying the enemy's industrial capacity to fight would not only shorten any future war but see the conflict won by bombing alone. They also believed that it would render the other services obsolescent.

Based on this doctrine, the RAF firmly embraced the strategic bomber and the fighter interceptor, the latter for defence against enemy bomber attacks. When it came to fighter defence, the British were well ahead of the Germans in September 1939 as they had created the world's first effective air defence system based on radar.

In this environment the RAF paid little heed to the needs of the British Army or Royal Navy. Few resources were allocated to support armies in the field and very little thought was given as to how aircraft could be used on the battlefield or overhead naval vessels sailing in enemy waters.

After the fall of Poland in September 1939, the British began sending forces to France in anticipation of the next German move. The Advanced Air Striking Force was formed (ten squadrons of Fairey Battles, two with Bristol Blenheims, four with Hawker Hurricanes and four with Westland Lysanders) and sent across the Channel. In name alone was this force in any way 'advanced', as it was largely equipped with single-engined Battle light bombers that proved a disaster once the *Blitzkrieg* was launched on 10 May 1940.

Time after time, the brave Battle and Blenheim crews were sent out without fighter protection and shot down in horrifying numbers. The result was a system of air support that was cumbersome, ineffective and devastatingly slow. Combined with the inept and criminal response from the French air force, the results were catastrophic. After the war it was revealed that the French had 1700 combat aircraft in the unoccupied southern zone and 2648 in North Africa. The failure of the two air forces to help stop the Wehrmacht from invading western Europe was one of the major contributing factors that led to the fall of France and the debacle at Dunkirk.

For the Germans it was a very different story. The Luftwaffe was designed from the outset to support the Wehrmacht directly, with its squadrons being equipped with a number of specialised aircraft. The most recognisable of these was the Junkers Ju 87 Stuka dive-bomber. The accuracy of the dive-bomber allowed it to attack pinpoint targets such as defensive forts, artillery positions, bridges and ships. It also had a terrifying effect on ground troops.

While the Stukas were attacking near the front, German medium bombers such as the Heinkel He 111, Dornier Do 17 and Junkers Ju 88 would be assigned to bigger targets such as railway stations, road junctions, supply depots and airfields. With targets softened up and the Allies in a state of disarray, Junkers Ju 52/3m transports would then fly in paratroopers and drop them en masse behind the frontline. These same aircraft were then re-roled as transports to fly in supplies required by fighter units in the field – drums of fuel, cases of ammunition and critical spare parts. All of these operations would be protected by both short-range Bf 109Es and long-range Bf 110C fighters.

This use of combined arms proved devastating to the Allies, and they would learn many lessons from the doomed defence of western Europe.

While the Germans had been victorious in Holland, Belgium and France, it came at a heavy price. No fewer than 1428 aircraft had been destroyed in France alone, this figure representing 28 percent of the Luftwaffe's then total strength. These losses came despite the Luftwaffe having enjoyed a degree of air superiority. The fact that the latter had not been complete was another lesson that the Allies took away with them from the Battle of France.

Although still convinced that strategic bombers would win the war, the RAF quickly realised that air support for the army had to be improved. After the Dunkirk evacuation, Air Marshal A S Barrett, commander of the RAF in France in 1940, was put in charge of a new force within the RAF – Army Cooperation Command.

Two veterans of the recent disaster in France, Brig J D Woodall and Grp Capt A Wann, were then given the task of studying the 'problem of air support to armies' and coming up with workable solutions. Wann and Woodall quickly identified the need for a tactical air force. This would be a strictly RAF formation designed and equipped to initially obtain air superiority over the battlefield and then attack ground targets in close cooperation with army forces.

In the autumn of 1940, between 5 September and 22 October, Wann and Woodall conducted a series of signal exercises and command and control trials in the quiet backwater of Northern Ireland. Their report highlighted the need for the creation of an elaborate system of radio links that would allow for the rapid passage of air support requests through a dedicated communications network, all outside the normal chains of command. This report, and the lessons learned up to this point in the war, formed the basis of what was to become the RAF's doctrine of air support.

In parallel with the Wann/Woodall report, developments in North Africa would also contribute greatly to the air support question. In the spring and summer months of 1941, and immediately after the two failed attempts to relieve the port of Tobruk in May and June of that year, two newly appointed air and land commanders – AVM Arthur Tedder and Gen Sir Claude Auchinleck – moved ahead with a series of conferences and exercises designed to solve problems of air support for ground forces. What resulted was a system similar to the Wann/Woodall report. Air Support Controls (ACS) were constructed and tested and fighter and bomber aircraft undertook a variety of tasks that were all designed to find their optimum role in air-to-ground operations. In combination these two developments led directly to the formation of the Desert Air Force – the Allies' first Tactical Air Force.

RAF historian Sir Maurice Dean identified three vital principles critical for effective army air cooperation. They were goodwill (a willingness to cooperate), sound tactics and excellent communications. By the summer of 1942 all three of these principles were being applied to great effect in the Western Desert. Ironically, back in Britain that cooperation and understanding between the Army and RAF was non-existent.

Some believed that the only solution was the creation of a separate army air force made up of specially designed aircraft that were all controlled by the army. All of the army's ideas were in direct violation of the RAF's first principles of air power – centralised command and concentration of force. Slowly but surely, however, support was growing for a mixed force of fighters, fighter-bombers, medium bombers and reconnaissance aircraft all under one air commander. The latter could then evaluate and assess the air and ground situation and apply the correct forces where needed. After a year of rancour and infighting, the new Air Expeditionary Force Headquarters was finally established in Fighter Command. Exercise *Spartan*, held in March 1943, showed how effective an RAF Composite Group really was.

In November 1943 the AEF was renamed the 2nd TAF, and it eventually included No 2 Group (which had been transferred from Bomber Command) and Nos 83 and 84 Groups. The RCAF's contribution to this new organisation was 12 squadrons under the command of No 83 Group. Three RCAF fighter wings (Nos 126, 127 and 144) equipped with Spitfires and one fighter-bomber wing (No 143) flying Typhoons would soon prove themselves in combat, contributing greatly to the overwhelming air superiority enjoyed by the Allies from D-Day right up until the end of the war.

MOBILE WING MAKE-UP

There were many reasons why the mobile air wing (a day-fighter wing consisted of three squadrons of 18 aircraft each with 39 officers and 743 other ranks – No 126 Wing would later grow to five squadrons) proved to be such a destructive and instrumental force on the battlefield. The first of these was, of course, its mobility. The ability to move as the army did and be close to the front was critical, so mobile wings had to be ready to change locations literally at a moment's notice, often at night, setting up shop at their new location and declaring themselves fully operational within just a matter of hours.

Opposite top
No 411 Sqn groundcrew enjoy a tea break during Exercise *Spartan* in March 1943. As part of this exercise, two opposing forces were organised as Eastland and Southland, with the former representing the Allies and the latter the Germans. The purpose of *Spartan* was to test the effectiveness of the tactical organisation that the RAF had put in place for the upcoming invasion of occupied Europe in June of the following year. The exercise lasted until 12 March, and it was deemed to be a success (*DND PI 15562*)

Opposite bottom
Part of Eastland's fighter defences were provided by these No 421 Sqn Spitfire VBs seen taxiing out at RAF Croughton, in Northamptonshire, during *Spartan*. Aircraft in the Eastland Force were painted with a white nose marking from the back of the spinner to the cockpit to help distinguish the opposing sides. Parked in front of the RCAF aircraft are the Spitfire IXs of No 124 Sqn (*DND PL 15556*)

EXERCISE *SPARTAN*

Exercise *Spartan* took place in the south of England in early March 1943. It was a large-scale exercise designed to sharpen the fighter and bomber groups destined for the invasion that was to take place in 1944. The opposing sides were listed as Eastland and Southland, with Southland representing the Germans. Each side had roughly the same number of squadrons, with 18-20 equipped with fighters, army support aircraft and light bombers.

The two air forces were, however, very different in the way they operated. The Eastland force employed 12 of its squadrons as 'mobile' units. This was designed to test the RAF participation in the exercise, evaluating how the mobile squadrons performed in the field. The exercise, which ran till 12 March, was deemed a success. While some of the composite groups involved had been hampered by inexperience (many were newly constituted), the overall structure had proven itself.

Prior to the exercise commencing, fighter, fighter-bomber, reconnaissance and light bomber units assigned to *Spartan* had been formed into wings that were in turn controlled by a group. Airfield Headquarters were also established as mobile organisations following the lessons learned during this exercise, and these could be moved from airfield to airfield at a moment's notice. Each Airfield Headquarters would normally control three squadrons, No 126 Airfield HQ, for example, being formed on 4 July 1943 at RAF Redhill, in Surrey, to control Nos 401, 411 and 412 Sqns of the Royal Canadian Air Force (RCAF). This organisation would subsequently be re-designated No 126 Wing at RAF Tangmere, in Sussex, on 15 May 1944.

Both the RAF and British Army were impressed with the results of Exercise *Spartan*, and they gave it their full endorsement. On 1 May the Chiefs of Staff approved the RAF's Air Expeditionary Force (AEF). The new AEF would provide a composite group for both the British and Canadian armies taking part in the coming invasion. The new composite groups were a mix of fighters, bombers and reconnaissance aircraft, and they were not fixed to a prescribed strength. Their command arrangement closely mirrored those established and proven by units assigned to the Desert Air Force, but it was larger and more sophisticated. In this system all air support requests were evaluated by the air commander, who gave priority to the objectives he believed were vital to winning the ground battle.

This meant the transportation of men, fuel, ammunition, food, clothing, spare parts and a vast array of other items.

Airfields also had to be either built from scratch or repaired – a tasked performed by engineers assigned to airfield Construction Wings. Their importance is revealed by the fact that they were some of the first support troops ashore on 7 June 1944.

All of this was backed up by Repair, Service and Salvage Units, which were responsible for major aircraft repairs and the collection of all 2nd TAF aircraft that crashed within Allied territory. Air Store Parks also played their part by issuing equipment and stores for frontline units, as did mobile radar units known as Group Control Centre (they provided radar coverage and control over the battlefield) and the RAF Regiment (responsible for airfield security, mine clearing and light anti-aircraft defences). This well orchestrated machine provided the mobile air wing with the vital supplies and aircraft needed for sustained air operations. For the most part this system worked as planned, and for the wings equipped with the Spitfire in particular this was critical.

The Vickers-Supermarine fighter was originally designed as a short-range interceptor – perfect for defending Britain in 1940, but a liability when the Allies went on the offensive following the D-Day landings. Even with the advent of new slipper drop tanks, the Spitfire's range was limited. Nevertheless, the vast majority of RAF and RCAF fighter units assigned to support the invasion of occupied Europe in the summer of 1944 were equipped with the Spitfire IX.

The aircraft's armament was also a cause for concern. Although its two 20 mm Hispano cannon packed a formidable punch against both aircraft and most ground targets, the relative ineffectiveness of the Spitfire's four 0.303-in Browning machine guns was well known in the RAF by this stage of the war. The fighter's ability as a ground attack platform was therefore rather limited. This failing had been recognised by Fighter Command, and before the invasion there was a big push to upgrade the Spitfire's armament to two 20 mm cannon and two 0.50-in machine guns. A portion of an official RAF report titled 'Loose Minute',

Spitfires of No 411 Sqn bask in the warm sunshine at B88 Heesch, in Holland, during the early spring of 1945. The pierced-steel planking (PSP) is clearly evident, with its straight lines and level surface. PSP has to go down as one of the greatest inventions of the war, as it allowed the Allies to turn almost any open, level, space into an instant airfield, thus making tactical air power possible (*Public Archives of Canada PA 115095*)

dated 29 March 1944, describes the urgency concerning this matter at the time;

'At the Commanders' meeting this morning the Air Commander-in-Chief (AC–in-C) directed that every possible effort was to be made to get into service in the shortest possible time the maximum number of Spitfires fitted with 0.50-in Browning guns. He also described that 2nd TAF was to ensure that adequate stocks of ammunition of the right type were provisioned. The AC-in-C said that this retrospective conversion was to be given high priority. It will mainly involve the Senior Technical Supply Office as soon as the appropriate technical leaflet has been published.'

Another 'Loose Minute' dated 12 March 1944 reveals figures related to the number of Spitfires already converted, and aircraft coming off the production lines;

'Air Commodore Battle, Chief Overseer, Ministry of Aircraft Production, rang to say that anticipated deliveries of 0.50-in Spitfire installations was as follows. For retrospective fitting – 80 sets in April and 80 sets in May. Off production already, 60 fitted in aircraft in March, 80 in April and 280 in May.'

In many respects the Spitfire IX was lightly armed when compared to the Typhoon (four 20 mm cannon) P-47D Thunderbolt (eight 0.50-in machine guns), P-38J Lightning (one 20 mm cannon and four 0.50-in machines guns) and P-51D Mustang (six 0.50-in machine guns), all of which were widely used by the Allies in western Europe as fighter-bombers. The Spitfire was also equipped to carry bombs and be used as a dive-bomber. Here again the British aircraft fell short of its contemporaries, however. All of the above fighters were capable of delivering 2000 lbs of bombs, whereas the Spitfire was only cleared to carry a 1000-lb load in September 1944! Air Fighting Development Unit Report No 141 describes the trials carried out to clear the Spitfire for heavier bomb loads;

SPITFIRE FITTED WITH THREE BOMB CARRIERS

Introduction – reference is made to Headquarters Air Defence of Great Britain letter reference ADGB/S32459/Air Tactics dated 10 July 1944, requesting that trials be carried out on a Spitfire carrying one 500-lb bomb under the belly and two 500-lb bombs on the wings.

1. **Spitfire IX NH251** was delivered from No 83 Group Support Unit on 11/7/44 without the necessary undercarriage modifications, which were carried out by this Unit. Trials were commenced on 29/7/44.

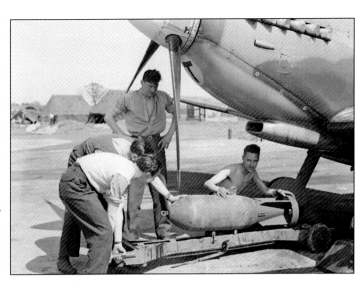

The Mk III MC 500-lb (227-kg) bomb was the principal air-to-ground weapon carried by the Spitfires of No 126 Wing. Unfortunately, this bomb, its fuses and tail assemblies were designed to be dropped horizontally, and the weapon was never intended to be delivered from an aircraft in a near vertical dive (*DND PL 29247*)

2. **Description** – the aircraft is a standard Spitfire IXE with Modification Spitfire/1209 incorporated. The oleo leg pressures are similar to those on standard Spitfire IXs and the tyre pressure remains standard at 57 lbs. The all-up weight carrying one 500-lb and two 250-lb bombs is 8480 lbs, which shifts the centre of gravity 4.9 ft aft.

3. **Limitations** – the following limitations have been imposed by Supermarine;

   (i) Aircraft is not to be landed over 8000 lbs, i.e. either the 500-lb bomb is jettisoned or 56 gallons of fuel consumed.

   (ii) Aircraft must operate from smooth surfaces, but see paragraph five below.

   (iii) No violent manoeuvres are to be carried out unless the 500-lb bomb is dropped or the 90-gallon drop tank emptied.

4. **Take-off** – permission was received to operate from this airfield, which has a rough grass surface. Take-off was made with the stick held back and the aircraft flown off the ground from a three-point position. No difficulty was experienced and no tendency to swing, or for a wing to drop immediately after take-off, was noticed. The take-off run increased, but by using +12 lbs of boost there is no appreciable difference in run over the normal Spitfire using +7 lbs of boost. The aircraft is slightly nose-heavy on take-off unless the elevator trim is set to neutral. Climbing speed is reached rather smoothly, but the initial climb can be safely made at 140 knots ASI.

5. **General Handling** – elevators and rudder remain effective, but the ailerons tend to become very sluggish above 20,000 ft. Little difference is made to the trim of the aircraft when any combination of bombs are released, and it is quite comfortable to fly the aircraft straight and level with one wing bomb on.

6. **Climb** – the maximum difference in the rate of climb at rated altitudes is 1250 ft/min, i.e. over a 5000 ft climb it takes some 20-25 seconds longer.

7. **Speed** – the reduction in speed at maximum cruising is some 23 mph, but at full throttle this is reduced to some 13 mph.

8. **Landing** – the landing with full bomb load should be made at an approach speed of 105-110 mph and carried out on three points so as to avoid bounce on rough surfaces. The aircraft touches down at about 70-80 mph and has a longer run.

9. **Armament Trials** – no trouble was experienced with the release of the bombs either in a salvo or singly in any normal dive-bombing attack.

10. **Dispersion** – when the bombs were released from a contacting height of 6500 ft in a salvo, the two 250-lb bombs fell on average within 19 yards of each other, and the 500-lb bomb within 90 yards of the two 250-lbs bombs. Over a number of releases made

during the course of the trial, consistent dispersions were duly noted.

11. **Conclusions** – the Spitfire IX modified to carry two 250-lb bombs and one 500-lb bomb is considered to be entirely satisfactory for operational use provided violent manoeuvres are not carried out prior to release of the 500-lb bomb. The aircraft can be operated from runways and grass surface airfields provided care is taken during take-off and the aircraft flown off from three points. Landing should not be attempted unless the 500-lb bomb has been released or 56 gallons of fuel is consumed. The average dispersion when all three bombs are released in a salvo is approximately 100 yards.

Fortunately for the RAF, the Spitfire design had the ability to be continuously developed and improved during the war. Other fighters were introduced, but few could match the Vickers-Supermarine design in terms of overall performance. One such aircraft was the Westland Whirlwind, of which just 112 examples were built in 1940 due to the unreliability of its twin Rolls-Royce Peregrine engines. The aircraft needed Merlins, but these were all allocated to Spitfires and Hurricanes. The Hawker Typhoon was also purchased as an eventual Spitfire replacement, but it too experienced a troubled development due to engine problems with its powerful, but temperamental, Napier Sabre and rear fuselage fragility.

Despite successors always appearing in the wings, the Spitfire remained a capable frontline interceptor (if not quite the best fighter-bomber) thanks to continuous upgrading programmes by Vickers-Supermarine and Rolls-Royce. In fact, by the time the Mk I entered service in June 1938, both companies had already started improving the airframe and increasing the power output of the Merlin engine. With the latter, as the horsepower increased, bringing better performance, so the Spitfire grew in weight. This in turn led to the adoption of a heavier propeller with more blades in order to better harness the power of the uprated Merlin. The airframe also had to be strengthened, adding still more weight.

While the Spitfire was continually improved, its contemporary, the Bf 109, went from bad to worse. With each increase in horsepower the Meserschmitt fighter's flying characteristics were degraded, and for novice pilots trying to master the skills required to both live and fight it was a devastating combination. By 1944 the Spitfire IX and Griffon-powered XIV equipped the majority of the RAF's fighter squadrons.

The Spitfire was asked to do many things during World War 2 – interceptor, air superiority fighter, fighter-bomber, tactical reconnaissance and carrier-borne fighter. When it came to pure air-to-air combat the Spitfire was supreme, but when saddled with bombs and sent on ground attack missions, the aircraft's performance was not nearly up to the job. It was in this scenario that the young pilots of No 126 Wing were tasked, and from D-Day until the end of the war they were able to compile a score – both in the air and on the ground – that was unmatched by any other wing on the continent.

FORMATION, D-DAY, BREAKOUT

No 126 Airfield HQ was formed on 4 July 1943 and consisted of No 401 'City of Westmount/Ram' Sqn, No 411 'Grizzly Bear' Sqn and No 412 'Falcon' Sqn. All three units were equipped with Spitfire VBs, although they had received Mk IXBs by November.

The war situation for the Allies by that time had begun to improve after the dark days of 1941-42. German expansion in the USSR had been checked, Axis forces had been driven out of North Africa and Sicily had been invaded. Planning for D-Day was also well underway.

The opposition that No 126 Airfield HQ would face on the other side of the English Channel took the form of Fw 190As and Bf 109Gs assigned to *Jagdgeschwader* 2 and 26, respectively – both very experienced units. Indeed, No 411 Sqn had Flg Off J R Spaetzel (in AB802) shot down and killed near Amiens when the unit was engaged by JG 26 on the very day No 126 Airfield HQ was formed. Sgt D H Stewart (in BM422) was wounded in the same action, but he returned to base. Jagdwaffe ranks would be progressively strengthened as more and more B-17s and B-24s of the USAAF's Eighth Air Force began to strike deeper into Germany.

Most of the operations mounted by No 126 Airfield HQ at this time consisted of bomber escort missions, codenamed 'Ramrods'. For the RCAF pilots involved, aerial victories were few and far between, but on 15 July No 411 Sqn's CO, Sqn Ldr G C Semple, registered No 126 Airfield HQ's first claim when he damaged an Fw 190 over Poix (in BL780). Flg Off H E Hamilton's fighter (BL972) was shot up in return, however. The only other loss for July was Spitfire VB EN784, flown by future ace Sqn Ldr George Keefer, CO of No 412 Sqn. His aircraft suffered an engine failure over the Channel during a 'Ramrod' and he bailed out. Keefer was quickly rescued.

In early August, No 126 Airfield HQ was ordered to a new location. Leaving behind the well-built hangars, runways and taxi tracks of RAF Redhill, the Canadian pilots found themselves flying from a grassy airfield in Staplehurst, Kent. Situated on low farmland, the new site left much to be desired. Mechanics were soon kept very busy repairing broken tail wheels caused by the hastily laid metal runway matting. Both pilots and groundcrew were now living under canvas – a state of affairs that they would have to get used to for the coming invasion.

August was a month of constant escort duties, with little to show for it. September would also prove to be a fallow month. Two Spitfires were lost to enemy action, however, in 24 hours on 18/19 September. BM199, flown by Flg Off J W Fiander of No 401 Sqn, suffered a glycol leak after being hit by flak near Dieppe. The pilot bailed out

In August 1943 No 126 Airfield HQ practised living under canvas at Staplehurst airfield in preparation for the invasion of France the following summer. Here, pilots from No 401 Sqn play cards as they wait for their next mission. In the foreground to the right is Flg Off William Klersy, who had joined the unit two months earlier. Later rising through the ranks to command the squadron during the final months of the war, Klersy would become No 126 Wing's second highest-scoring ace with 14.5 victories, three damaged and two destroyed on the ground. His ground attack efforts also resulted in him claiming 90 vehicles, eight locomotives and eight railway goods trucks destroyed. Having survived the war in Europe, 22-year-old Klersy perished in a flying accident on 22 May 1945 (*Public Archives of Canada PL 22010*)

over the Channel and was retrieved by an air-sea rescue (ASR) Walrus. The following day Flt Lt V A Haw of No 411 Sqn was downed (in BL422) by an Fw 190 from III./JG 26 near Courtrai, the pilot becoming a prisoner of war (PoW). Finally, Sqn Ldr I C Ormston of No 411 Sqn was also forced to abandon his Spitfire (BM627) over the water on 26 September when it too suffered engine failure. An ASR Walrus came to his aid as well.

The Canadians would have to wait until 1 October to avenge these losses, No 126 Airfield HQ finally tallying its first victories during 'Ramrod 258' when it escorted a force of 12 Boston light bombers from No 107 Sqn that were targeting a power station in Orleans. No 412 Sqn provided the escort, and Flt Sgt Harlow Bowker (in BL425) claimed two Fw 190s downed over Abbeville. Flg Off D J Dewan (in AR395) was credited with damaging a third Focke-Wulf.

Several days earlier more good news had reached No 126 Airfield HQ – it would be moving to RAF Biggin Hill, also in Kent. The announcement was a major morale booster, for Biggin Hill was the RAF's most advanced and prestigious airfield, boasting accommodation for both pilots and groundcrews. The unit arrived on 13 October, and once settled in No 126 Airfield HQ was soon back in the air.

2nd TAF's systematic attack on targets in France and the Low Countries continued throughout this period. 12 November would see No 126 Airfield HQ score again, but this time on the ground. Two Spitfires from No 412 Sqn set off on a 'Rhubarb' (small attack by fighters with the object of destroying enemy aircraft in the air or on the ground, or striking at ground targets), and this time newly promoted Plt Off Harlow Bowker (in BL425) destroyed a Bf 109 on the ground near Lille, although he was in turn wounded in the neck by flak.

On 15 November the 2nd TAF was officially proclaimed under the command of Air Marshal Sir Arthur Coningham, previously C-in-C of the Western Desert Air Force during 1942. As the 2nd TAF came into being, it quickly grew in size with the formation of several new airfield HQs and wings. The 2nd TAF consisted of three groups when it formed – Nos 2, 83 and 84 Groups, as well as the 2nd TAF HQ. No 126 Airfield HQ was under the command of No 83 Group.

Initially, operations for No 83 Group remained the same as before. Railway marshalling yards, industrial sites and Luftwaffe airfields in France continued to be the main targets, with No 126 Airfield HQ providing the usual fighter escort. Preparations for the coming invasion were also taking place, with squadrons being systematically withdrawn from operations to attend Armament Practice Camp (APC) courses. There, the Spitfire units could hone their air-to-air and air-to-ground gunnery skills and practise the fine art of dive-bombing. Courses

Flt Lt J E Sheppard made No 401 Sqn's first claim – an Fw 190 shot down over Achiel airfield – as part of No 126 Airfield HQ on 26 November 1943 while escorting USAAF B-26s that had been sent to attack targets in the Cambrai area. Prior to joining No 401 Sqn in February 1943, Sheppard had served for a year in the Merchant Ship Fighter Unit, which flew rocket-launched Hurricanes from specially modified merchant vessels sailing as part of the Atlantic convoys. Surviving a crash into the sea in February 1942, Sheppard would both 'make ace' and command No 412 Sqn between April and August 1944 (*DND PL 22012*)

usually lasted between five and twenty-one days. Curiously, No 126 Airfield HQ's APC saw its pilots trained in gunnery and rocket firing at RAF Fairwood Common, in Wales, but no dive-bombing instruction was given whatsoever!

On 23 November No 411 Sqn suffered No 126 Airfield HQ's first fatality in more than four months when Flt Sgt S M Kent suffered engine failure while changing tanks in Spitfire IX MA312 during 'Ramrod 326' and his aircraft crashed into the Channel.

All three squadrons would see action between 26 November and 1 December, as USAAF B-26s targeted enemy installations in France and Belgium. An Fw 190 was destroyed by future ace Flt Lt Jackson Sheppard (in MJ146) on the 26th, although MH886 was written off in a crash-landing at RAF Hawkinge, in Kent, after being shot up in the same engagement – Flt Lt T Koch survived unscathed.

Three days later No 126 Airfield HQ provided escort for 72 B-26s attacking Chièvres airfield, in Belgium. No 412 Sqn was in the top cover position, and it was bounced by ten Fw 190s. Flt Lt A C Coles (in MJ169) managed to attack one of the fighters, which he saw going down trailing smoke, but he was in turn shot down by another Fw 190 near Dunkirk. Coles was captured and his Fw 190 listed as damaged. Squadronmate Flg Off J A Robertson (in MJ331) was not so lucky, for he was shot down and killed near Ypres. Finally, Flt Lt D S Wurtele (in MJ312) limped back to base with a shot up Spitfire.

Both Nos 401 and 411 Sqns also 'mixed it' with the Fw 190s during this engagement, Flg Off L M Cameron (in MH845) of the former unit and Flt Lt D R Matheson (in MI850) of the latter squadron each being credited with a victory.

Flg Off L M Cameron poses for the camera during his tour with No 402 Sqn in July 1942. Having completed his service with this unit in April 1943, he then spent six months as an instructor, before being posted to No 401 Sqn in November. Cameron became a flight commander the following month, and 18 days later was promoted to CO. Between 29 November 1943 and 7 June 1944 he claimed five enemy aircraft shot down and one damaged to add to his previous one destroyed and one damaged from his time with No 402 Sqn. Cameron was also credited with 75 vehicles and five locomotives destroyed. On 3 July 1944 he was shot down by flak, and after two months in hiding Cameron was eventually captured. However, he managed to escape and eventually returned to the UK in September of that year (*DND PL 10403*)

On 30 November No 401 Sqn escorted USAAF B-17s on a 'Ramrod' and lost two Spitfires to engine failure. Flt Lt A E Studholme (in MH 911) became a PoW after he bailed out off the Dutch coast, while Flt Lt H D MacDonald (an ace with seven and two shared kills to his name) perished when his fighter (MJ115) crashed into the sea off Essex. He had only just started his third tour, joining No 401 Sqn on 28 October. More losses came the following day when No 411 Sqn escorted 72 B-26s on a morning 'Ramrod'. Flt Lt D R Matheson (in MJ236) claimed an Fw 190 destroyed over Cambrai but was then forced to bail out into captivity. Squadronmate Plt Off J A St Denis (in MJ288) was also downed in the same area, although he was killed. A second Fw 190 victory was credited to Flg Off S A Mills (in MH850). An afternoon sweep saw Sqn Ldr Keefer of No 412 Sqn claim an Fw 190 as a probable.

The last major action involving No 126 Airfield HQ aircraft took place on 20 December when a raid by Eighth Air Force heavy bombers on Bremen, in Germany, was supported by diversionary attacks provided by No 11 Group and the Ninth Air Force. An impressive force of 211 B-26s, 60 Mitchells, 37 Bostons, 415 Spitfires, 155 Typhoons and 20 Hurricanes took part. No 126 Airfield HQ did not participate directly in this operation, but at approximately the same time its trio of squadrons flew a fighter sweep over the Rijen-Brussels area, where a Do 217 was shot down by No 411 Sqn pilots Flg Off D J Givens (in MJ295) and Plt Off L A Dunn (in MJ283). Five minutes later Flt Lt L M Cameron (serial unknown) of No 401 Sqn shot down a Ju 88 near Lille. These victories were overshadowed by the loss of three No 401 Sqn pilots, however. Flt Lt R J Buckles (in EN629) was shot down by return fire from the Ju 88, while Flg Off N W Maybee (in MH845) and Sgt J J Morrissey (in MJ172) collided over Gravelines and bailed out into captivity.

An American in the RCAF, Sqn Ldr Joe McFarlane took over as OC No 411 Sqn after Sqn Ldr I C Ormston was injured in a flying accident on 21 December 1943 (*Public Archives of Canada*)

The following day Sqn Ldr I C Ormston (in MJ287) was badly injured when his Spitfire suffered engine failure shortly after take-off and his fighter crashed near RAF Biggin Hill. He was replaced as CO of the unit by American Sqn Ldr J D McFarlane.

30 December would see the last victory scored by Canada's greatest ace, Flt Lt George Beurling, who had joined No 412 Sqn as a flight

Canada's ace of aces, Flg Off George Beurling, adds the finishing touches to his victory tally on Spitfire IXB MA585 after claiming his 30th kill on 24 September 1943. Assigned to No 403 Sqn at the time, he joined No 412 Sqn as a flight commander the following month, and downed his 31st, and last, victory with the unit on 30 December while flying Spitfire IXB MH883 (*via Bruce Robertson*)

In this case the Tiger Moth's bark was certainly worse then any bite. No 401 Sqn's 'hack' is seen here being warmed up for another 'mission'. Each squadron was equipped with a single Tiger Moth or Auster III aircraft for communications duties. No 412 Sqn's Tiger Moth was routinely 'stunted' by a bored Flt Lt Beurling at Biggin Hill until No 126 Airfield HQ CO Wg Cdr 'Buck' McNair forbade him from flying it! (*Public Archives of Canada PMR 77-611*)

commander in late November in an effort to boost the experience level in the unit. Known as 'Buzz' or 'Screwball', he had claimed 29 victories during the defence of Malta to end the campaign as its leading ace. Providing escort with the rest of his unit for a group of B-17s sent to bomb targets in the Compeigne area, Beurling and his flight intercepted Fw 190s that were attempting to engage the USAAF 'heavies'. Beurling shot one of the fighters down to take his final tally to 31 and 1 shared destroyed, having claimed an Fw 190 with No 403 Sqn on 24 September. His relationship with No 126 Airfield HQ CO, and fellow ace, Wg Cdr R W 'Buck' McNair soon deteriorated, however, and Beurling was posted back to Canada in April 1944.

Always a loner in the air, and overtly rebellious on the ground, Beurling had pushed McNair's patience too far when, forbidden to fly the unit's Tiger Moth (he revelled in 'stunting' in the biplane overhead the airfield), he decided to race station transport around the tarmac! McNair confronted Beurling and told him that if had not packed up his things and left the base within the hour he would physically remove him.

NEW YEAR

January 1944 through to the invasion in June would see No 126 Airfield HQ flying and fighting as before, but generally with little to show for their efforts in terms of aerial victories. Claims were few and far between, but the variety of enemy aircraft shot down was impressive – 13 Fw 190s, two Bf 110 nightfighters, one 'Me 210' (almost certainly an Me 410) and one Ju 88. The first success came on 6 January when Nos 401 and

411 Sqns flew a sweep during a 'Noball' anti-V1 attack by No 2 Group Mitchells and Mosquitos. Bounced by Bf 109Gs and Fw 190s, Flg Off H K Hamilton (in MH885) of No 401 Sqn claimed a Focke-Wulf destroyed, as did Flt Lt R W Orr (in MJ229) of No 411 Sqn.

Three days later No 401 Sqn suffered No 126 Airfield HQ's first lost of 1944 when American Flg Off R M Davenport (in MH827) was shot down by flak during a 'Rhubarb' in the Hesdin area. He evaded successfully, however. Two more aircraft succumbed to engine failure on 24 and 28 January during 'Ramrods', both fighters (No 401 Sqn's MJ145 on the 24th and No 412 Sqn's MJ302 on the 28th) crashing in the Channel. Fortunately, Flt Lts J Sheppard and D G McKay were quickly rescued.

14 February proved to be a day of mixed emotions for No 126 Airfield HQ, as at 1605 hrs Flg Off Z J Zabek of No 412 Sqn was killed when MH734 suffered engine failure over Knockholt, in Kent, and crashed. Ten minutes later, eight Spitfires from No 401 Sqn intercepted a lone 'Me 210' (again probably an Me 410) taking off from St Andre airfield during a 'Ranger'. Flg Off R K Hayward (in MJ124) shot the aircraft down.

No 412 Sqn's Flt Lt A B W Ketterson (in MJ306) was killed on 4 March when his fighter crashed near Ypres during 'Ramrod 623', again probably because of engine failure. On the 7th No 401 Sqn escorted 108 B-26s to Creil marshalling yards, where two Fw 190s of 12./JG 2 were intercepted at low-level and downed by Flt Lt J E Sheppard (in MJ246) and Flg Off W T Klersy (in MJ289). Two Bf 109s were also claimed as damaged.

No 401 Sqn enjoyed No 126 Airfield HQ's best day to date in terms of aerial victories on 15 March when it joined units from No 127 Airfield HQ in an escort mission for 72 B-26s bombing Aulony marshalling yards. Having lost Flg Off R J F Sherk (in MJ126) near Cambrai to engine trouble – JG 26 claimed him as shot down, and Sherk successfully evaded – six Fw 190s were spotted 'attempting to land' on a runway at Cambrai airfield that was blocked by an Me 410. The No 401 Sqn pilots dove into the attack, and Flt Lts J E Sheppard (in MJ246) and A F Halcrow (in MH724) and Flg Offs R K Hayward (in MJ124) and D D Ashleigh (in MJ119) shot down four Fw 190s and damaged the Me 410. The Focke-Wulfs were from 7./JG 26, and they were in fact forming up for a flight to Rheine and not attempting to land. They had not been warned of the approaching Spitfires.

Engine unreliability cost No 126 Airfield HQ two more Spitfires the following day during 'Ramrod 661', No 401 Sqn's Plt Off K B Woodhouse evading after bailing out of MJ119 southeast of Amiens, and No 412 Sqn's Flg Off T M Saunderson being rescued by an

Flt Lt R W Orr of No 411 Sqn was one of the unit's more successful pilots prior to the D-Day invasion. Indeed, between 6 January and 7 May 1944 he shot down three Fw 190s. On 2 June Orr was hit by flak and forced to bail out over the Channel, although he was quickly retrieved and returned to his unit (*DND PL 28257*)

ASR Walrus after he suffered mechanical problems in MJ149 over the Somme Estuary.

It was No 412 Sqn that succeeded in claiming No 126 Airfield HQ's next kill too when, on 23 March, Flg Off D C Laubman (in MJ230) and Flt Lt W B Needham (in MK622) spotted a Ju 88 below them whilst escorting 72 B-26s to the Creil marshalling yards. Laubman's fighter was hit by defensive fire during the engagement, causing him to crash-land at RAF Kenley. Needham finished the German bomber off, however.

By April 1944 the full weight of the combined bomber offensive by the Tactical Air Forces, the US Eighth and Fifteenth Air Forces and Bomber Command began to show impressive results. The introduction of effective escort fighters (P-51B/Cs, P-47Ds and P-38Js) in growing numbers by the Americans had a disastrous effect on the Luftwaffe's fighter defences. Many of the great *Experten* of the 1940-43 period had fallen victim to the escorts, and replacement pilots were not up to early war standards. Flight training had been accelerated and compressed due to a shortage of fuel and the desperate military situation now facing the Germans. The new pilots had little impact, therefore, instead providing their well-trained Canadian counterparts with easy targets.

Consequently, Luftwaffe fighter units from all fronts were pulled back into Germany proper. This move out of France soon became obvious to the pilots of 2nd TAF as fewer and fewer enemy fighters were now being encountered during missions over occupied western Europe. This 'dry spell' was even more telling in the two months leading up to the invasion.

All three squadrons within No 126 Airfield HQ moved from RAF Biggin Hill to RAF Tangmere, via a ten-day APC at RAF Fairwood Common, during March-April. In this brief time out of the frontline, pilots were taught dive-bombing skills in the Spitfire IX, prior to heading for their new base in Sussex.

No 126 Airfield HQ's first aerial victory in more than a month came on 23 April when, during an evening 'Ranger', No 401 Sqn caught two Bf 110Gs of 8./NJG 4 up near Laon at 1945 hrs. Flg Offs R K Hayward (in MJ982) and D D Ashleigh (in MJ385) shared in the destruction of one of the nightfighters, while Plt Off Dowbiggin (in MH483) got the other one. In a portent of things to come, earlier that same day No 411 Sqn had undertaken its first bombing mission when it had attacked the Merville Viaduct.

Nos 401 and 411 Sqns targeted the railway bridge at Granville four days later, and lost two Spitfires and a pilot in the process. The former unit's Flg Off W E Cummings (in MJ982) was killed when his machine hit the ground during a low-level attack on the target, while Flg Off C D Cross (in MJ140) of No 411 Sqn was injured when he bailed out of his flak-damaged fighter off Selsey. Cross was rescued by a Royal Navy corvette. No 401 Sqn's Flt Lt T Koch (in MH841) was also injured when he crash-landed near Worthing after running out of fuel at the end of an escort mission on 2 May.

Five days later No 411 Sqn's Flt Lt R W Orr (in MJ229) took his tally of victories to three when he downed two Fw 190s from 3./JG 26 that had just been scrambled from Laon/Athies airfield. No 126 Airfield HQ had been given the job of escorting B-17s and B-24s

No 412 Sqn's Flg Off Donald Laubman joined the unit in August 1943, having previously served with the RCAF's No 133 Sqn in Canada. By the time he ended his tour with No 412 Sqn in November 1944 he had become the 2nd TAF's leading ace with 14 and 2 destroyed and 3 damaged. All of these successes occurred over the continent after D-Day except for a Bf 109 he damaged on 30 December 1943 and a shared victory over a Ju 88 on 23 March 1944. Having been rested from operations, Laubman joined No 402 Sqn as its CO on 7 April 1945. Exactly a week later he was shot down by flak, spending the closing days of the war as a PoW (*DND PMR 78-306*)

targeting Laon, and the two downed German fighters were intercepted as they took off to engage the bombers. These successes were tempered by the loss of No 401 Sqn's Plt Off T W Dowbiggin (in MH483), whose engine failed when he tried to switch fuel tanks near Laon. After belly landing, the Canadian was quickly captured. His virtually intact fighter was destroyed in a series of strafing passes by Sqn Ldr M Cameron and his wingman.

10 May proved to be a day of heavy action for the 2nd TAF in general and No 126 Airfield HQ in particular. No 412 Sqn flew a sweep over the Rheims area in the early afternoon and encountered Fw 190s from I./JG 2. Sqn Ldr J E Sheppard (in MH826) and Flt Lt E C R Likeness (in MH617) each claimed one destroyed, but the latter pilot was then forced to bail out into captivity after his fighter was shot up by another Focke-Wulf. Flt Lt J A C Crimmins (in MK853) also fell victim to the Fw 190s, being killed when his Spitfire crashed near Rheims. No 126 Airfield HQ lost a second Spitfire and its pilot that evening when No 401 Sqn undertook a sweep of St Omer and was engaged by Bf 109Gs. Flg Off H K Hamilton (in MJ385) claimed to have damaged one of the enemy fighters, but his aircraft was then hit by flak and he bailed out. Hamilton was also captured.

The following day No 412 Sqn lost two aircraft over the Pas de Calais during 'Ramrod 867' when they collided. Flg Off R W Thatcher (in MH427) ditched and was rescued, while Flg Off J S Hamilton (in MJ136) took to his parachute and was also recovered.

On 12 May No 126 Airfield HQ (along with all the other Airfield HQs in the 2nd TAF) was reorganised as a wing. Nothing really changed except for administrative purposes. Fighter Command's 'big wings' were re-titled Sectors and the Airfield HQs became wings. As previously mentioned, the newly minted No 126 Wing was by now based at Tangmere, living under canvas. This was all in preparation for the coming invasion, and the nomadic life the outfit would lead on the continent.

Despite the redesignation, sweeps were performed as before for the three Canadian units, and losses continued to mount. 15 May saw No 411 Sqn conduct a morning sweep of Amiens that resulted in Flt Lt S A Mills (in MJ831) being shot down by flak over the target area. He was made a PoW. Four days later No 411 Sqn suffered a particularly heavy blow when its CO, Sqn Ldr Norm Fowlow (in MK834), was killed during a dive-bombing attack on Neufchatel. Flak hit the bomb carried on the fighter's centreline and the weapon exploded. Fowlow, who had only assumed command of No 411 Sqn the previous month, was replaced by future ace Sqn Ldr Graham Robertson.

Fellow ace, and unit CO, Sqn Ldr L M Cameron (in MJ131) of No 401 Sqn took his tally to four kills on 24 May when he claimed an Fw 190 destroyed over Nivelles following an evening bomber escort mission. Having seen his charges safely over water after a raid on Lille/Vendeville airfield, Cameron took his unit down to strafe trains, at which point he spotted the lone Fw 190 and duly shot it down.

'Ramrod 960' on 2 June saw Flt Lt R W Orr (in MJ229) forced to bail out over the Channel after his fighter was struck by flak. Orr, who

would subsequently claim three victories and two damaged after No 126 Wing moved to the Continent, was rescued. Squadronmate Flg Off C B Cohen (in MK840) was not so lucky 24 hours later when he bailed out of his flak-damaged Spitfire too low and drowned. His unit had been on a sweep of the Argentan/Cherbourg area.

Flg Off Cohen would prove to be No 126 Wing's final casualty pre-D-Day, for on 4 June all three units were kept busy preparing their aircraft for the long awaited invasion of France – originally scheduled for the following day, but postponed 24 hours due to poor weather. Part of those preparations would see all of the wing's Spitfire IXs marked with distinctive black and white 'Invasion stripes', applied in great haste in distemper.

D-DAY

Preparing for D-Day had been a long and arduous process. The Allied air forces facing the Germans were in every respect overwhelming, and each by themselves were numerically superior to anything the Luftwaffe could put into the field. Allied fighter strength alone on D-Day numbered 4100 aircraft, of which 1800 (mostly Spitfire IXs) were assigned to the RAF. German fighter strength for Normandy numbered in the low hundreds, with just 425 Bf 109Gs and Fw 190s of which between 250-280 were serviceable on any given day.

By 1944 the Luftwaffe in many ways was fighting three separate air wars. The first and most destructive was the high altitude Allied Strategic Bombing campaign. To fight the predominantly USAAF daylight raiders the Germans could muster close to 850 single-seat fighters. On the Eastern front, they were battling the Soviet tactical air forces with approximately 515 fighters. Finally, in the night skies they

On the eve of the Normandy Invasion D-Day stripes are hastily applied to a No 411 Sqn Spitfire at RAF Tangmere, in Sussex. These high-visibility markings were designed to make Allied aircraft 'easier' to identify over the landing beaches for Allied naval and army anti-aircraft gunners (*DND PL 30827*)

had a force of 572 mostly twin-engined nightfighters that were attempting to counter RAF Bomber Command.

By comparison, 2nd TAF alone had 53 squadrons of fighters and fighter-bombers, six of which were equipped with nightfighters by D-Day. Allied fighter strength was now greater than the entire operational strength of the Luftwaffe at the time of the German invasion of Holland, Belgium and France in the Spring of 1940!

It must also be noted that the Luftwaffe was no longer an offensive fighting force. Its role was now purely defensive. In some aspects it was still effective, but for all intents and purposes the Luftwaffe was a spent force. Many of the veteran pilots had been killed or wounded, and the ones that had survived were fighting just to stay alive by the summer of 1944. Often outnumbered, they fought a hopeless rearguard action. The new and inexperienced replacements rushed to the front did not last long, and German reports indicated that 20 to 30 of these young men would be lost for every Allied aircraft shot down. Groundcrews were also being stripped from their units and pressed into service in the infantry, causing serviceability rates to drop.

By contrast, the pilots of No 126 Wing had a definite edge in both training and combat experience. During the mid-war years, the losses suffered within RAF fighter ranks had been relatively light. This was due in part to the Spitfire's short range, which meant that many escort missions were restricted to targets in western France and the Low Countries, where German response was both limited and infrequent. In fact flak posed a greater threat than the Jagdwaffe.

Many pilots flew on operations for lengthy periods, and a high proportion of the squadron and flight commanders were on their second or third tours by D-Day. For the Canadians, home defence pilots had been redeployed to the UK in substantial numbers, as had former instructors. Both had been released for operational service due to the fact that the potential for a Japanese attack on the west coast of Canada had all but disappeared due to Allied victories in the Pacific.

On the eve of D-Day No 126 Wing was more than ready. Since its inception on 4 July 1943, No 126 Airfield HQ/Wing had amassed a modest score of just 29 aerial victories. With D-Day at hand the wing would at last be able to take the fight to the enemy both in the air and on the ground.

On the first day of the invasion the patrols flown by No 126 Wing proved to be both uneventful and disappointing. However, to see Allied troops going ashore was a great relief for the Canadian pilots following months of bomber escort missions, exercises and seemingly endless rehearsals for D-Day. In the bigger picture, these sweeps on 6 June 1944 were part of the incredible 1547 fighter sorties flown by the Allied Expeditionary Air Force on that historic day.

As part of the Allied plan, 36 fighters would remain on station overhead the British and Canadian beaches, with a similar number over the American beaches, throughout the hours of daylight. A further 1800 sorties were flown by the fighter units as they escorted Allied bombers and troop carriers operating over Normandy. By the end of the day 2nd TAF fighters had claimed four Ju 88s and three Fw 190s shot down for the loss of 20 assorted fighter and bomber types to both German fighters and flak.

While the pilots of No 126 Wing may have been disappointed with the lack of 'activity' that they encountered on 6 June, the lacklustre response by the Luftwaffe to the invasion was a clear vindication of the Allied strategy in the build up to D-Day. The day and night bombing campaign by the Eighth and Fifteenth Air Forces, Bomber Command and the 2nd TAF had drawn the Jagdwaffe into a battle of attrition that it could not win. The Allied bombing attacks on Luftwaffe airfields in Normandy prior to the invasion had also forced the Germans to disperse their units from the immediate coastal area. The air superiority enjoyed by the Allies over the invasion beachhead was as close to perfection as one could get. German fighter pilot claims for D-Day amounted to just 20+ aircraft shot down, despite the skies over Normandy being literally filled with thousands of Allied machines.

7 June would prove to be a far more productive day for the eager pilots of No 126 Wing. As the beachhead expanded and new units poured ashore, 2nd TAF Typhoons began to hit more and more ground targets. Overhead, Spitfires continued their patrols and began to encounter the Luftwaffe more frequently as German units were posted into the area. The pilots of No 401 Sqn opened the scoring for the wing at 0920 hrs when 12+ Ju 88C-6 long-range fighters of I./ZG 1 attempted to attack the invasion fleet – the Brittany-based unit had lost four aircraft the previous day in an identical attack. The first Ju 88 to come down hit a balloon cable and crashed, at which point a dozen more appeared out of the clouds and dove for the beaches below. The pilots of No 401 Sqn attacked at once, but their attempt at interception was 'interfered with' by some USAAF P-47s.

No 412 Sqn now joined the fray, while No 411 Sqn remained as top cover. In the next few minutes eight of the intruders were claimed to have been shot down, two of them falling to No 401 Sqn CO Sqn Ldr L M Cameron (in MJ131) to take his final tally to six destroyed and two damaged. Wing Leader Wg Cdr George Keefer (in MK826) also got one to give him ace status too. No 401 Sqn's other kills fell to Flg Off D F Husband (in MJ289), Flt Lt R H Cull (in MK300), Flg Off G D Billings (in ML135), Flt Lt G B Murray (in MJ246) and Flg Off W A Bishop (in MH774), with the latter two sharing a bomber between them. Future ace Flg Off P M Charron (in MJ485) of No 412 Sqn also destroyed a Ju 88 in this action.

No 126 Wing flew its second patrol starting at 1300 hrs, and 30 minutes into the mission bomb-equipped Fw 190s (possibly from III./JG 54) were spotted and attacked. Making his second claim of the day, Wg Cdr George Keefer (again in MK826) shot down one of the fighters, as did future ace Flg Off Bill Klersy (in MJ289) of No 401 Sqn. Three more were believed to have been damaged by squadron pilots. Plt Off N Marshall (in MK902) of No 401 Sqn failed to return to Tangmere following this mission, however, having been shot down and killed by either flak or fighters.

No 126 Wing's third and final patrol of the day took place from 1900 hrs, and No 411 Sqn's CO Sqn Ldr G D Robertson (in MK885) and squadronmate, and future ace, Flt Lt G W Johnson (in MH754) each claimed a Bf 109G destroyed just north of Caen.

By day's end No 126 Wing had claimed 12 aircraft shot down, which reflected the level of combat experienced by 2nd TAF units as a whole on 7 June. Indeed, it had lost 18 Spitfires and Seafires, 12 Typhoons and six Mustang IIIs. The USAAF had also suffered considerable losses, with 30 P-47s, 13 P-51s and a P-38 being destroyed in combat.

NEW AIRFIELDS

As the beachhead was expanded and the aerial battles raged overhead, building landing strips within the newly liberated territory was an immediate priority. As a result airfield construction wings were amongst the first support troops ashore on 7 June. Work began immediately, with bulldozers and graders breaking the ground at Ste Croix-sur-Mer. First to be constructed were Emergency Landing Strips (ELS) where aircraft in trouble could land. Next in line were the refuelling and re-arming (R&R) strips and, finally, the advanced landing grounds (ALG). The latter were established for occupation by full-strength fighter units, and this meant that the runways at ALGs had to be 1200 yards long and covered with either square mesh track (SMT) or pierced-steel planking (PSP).

While the pilots of No 126 Wing were doing their job defending the beaches of Normandy, the mobile ground elements of the wing were making their way to France. Its advance party had left Tangmere on 31 May and arrived at the assembly area at RAF Old Sarum, in Wiltshire, later that same day. There, vehicles were waterproofed and made ready for the Channel crossing. On 4 June the party was told that they would be moving very soon, with new identity cards being issued and each man receiving a pound note in advance pay, which was quickly exchanged for French francs. The following day they moved to Camp A19 near Druxford, in Hampshire, and on 6 June the men received their overnight packs and life belts, prior to being transported to Portsmouth. At 1300 hrs the ships began to assemble in convoy, before setting off for France.

The first RCAF ground officer to set foot on French soil, at Ver-sur-Mer, was No 126 Wing's Intelligence Officer Monty Berger at dawn on 7 June. Once on firm ground, the advance party immediately set off for Ste Croix-sur-Mer – site of B3 ALG.

In order to move No 126 Wing across the Channel it was divided into several parties. First ashore was the so-called 'increment' to 'A' Party, which consisted of 33 officers and men. It landed at first light on 7 June and proceeded the next day to Ste Croix-sur-Mer, where B3 was being constructed. This was followed by the rest of 'A'

2nd TAF vehicles and equipment leave Portsmouth naval dockyard for Normandy on the afternoon of 6 June 1944. Logistics played a huge role in the success of the mobile fighter wing, with groundcrew and other support staff being the unsung heroes of the Allied effort during World War 2. This photograph shows a mixed bag of transports, including many examples of the ubiquitous Jeep – all of which have been marked with an RAF roundel (*Public Archives of Canada PL 30236*)

Party (18 officers and men) on 8 June. By the afternoon of the 9th aircraft had started using B3. On 15 June 'A' Party moved to a new site at Bény-sur-Mer to establish B4. The final element – 'B' Party of more than 1000 officers and men – made their way to B4 and became fully operational on 18 June.

As elements of No 126 Wing headed for their new landing ground, the Luftwaffe was pouring additional units into the battle area too. Bombers from southern France and Italy arrived and fighters from Home Defence units were flown in to bring the total available strength to about 1000 aircraft. Despite this increase, it was not until the evening of 10 June that No 126 Wing scored again. Mounting a patrol over Evreux, Chartres and Argentan, a single Fw 190 was spotted and shot down by No 401 Sqn's Flt Lt A A Williams (in MJ289) and No 411 Sqn's Flt Lt H J Nixon (in MJ295). No 412 Sqn's only event of note on this day was Plt Off D R C Jamieson's force-landing in MJ136 south of Tilly-sur-Suelles after it suffered a glycol leak.

The following day No 126 Wing experienced two more losses, one of which resulted in the unit's first fatality over Normandy. No 411 Sqn's Flt Sgt T W Tuttle (in NH195) perished on just his third mission when his fighter was brought down by flak at Villons les Buissons. Flt Lt H G Garwood (in MJ255) force-landed near Tilly-sur-Suelles when his aircraft suffered an engine failure.

By 13 June landing strips' B2 Bazenville and B3 Ste Croix-sur-Mer were ready for use, and during the early morning Spitfires from No 126 Wing flew into the latter strip. They would use this site during the day, before returning to Tangmere prior to nightfall. By sunset on 12 June the third wave of Allied troops had come ashore and were taking the attack to the Germans. More than 325,000 troops, 104,000 tons of supplies

One of the first priorities of the Allied armies shortly after D-Day was the construction of airfields within the beachhead, and this in turn meant that personnel from the RAF Airfield Construction Service (ACS) were some of the first troops ashore on 7 June. Here, ACS crews are securing rolls of square mesh track. The first airfields constructed were Emergency Landing Strips, followed by Refuelling and Rearming Strips and, finally, Advanced Landing Grounds (*Author's Collection*)

ADVANCED LANDING GROUNDS

The effectiveness of the 2nd TAF would hinge on the quality of these new airfields, for without them the RAF and USAAF would struggle to provide ground forces with the tactical air support they required to successfully break out of the beachhead at Normandy. Prior to the invasion, no fewer than 23 ALGs were constructed in southern England in preparation for D-Day. This put the fighter-bombers closer to landing beaches and provided good practice for the construction crews.

So important were these future airfields that engineers of the RAF Airfield Construction Service (ACS) were among those in the first assault waves.

Their job was to construct ALGs as fast as possible so that the fighter-bomber wings could operate from airfields within a radius of 100 miles of the frontline. In all 20 airfields were established in the British Sector. By September 1944 a total of 76 airfields had been constructed, and the ACS numbered more than 20,000 men.

Captured German airfields were used whenever possible and, surprisingly, they could be rehabilitated and made operational sooner than new airfields. This 'recycling' of bases became the preferred method as Allied forces entered Germany.

and 54,000 vehicles were now in France. Operation *Overlord* had been a success. The beachhead was firmly established, but still hazardous.

All three units assigned to No 126 Wing soon got used to flying from B3, although No 412 Sqn's Flt Lt R I A Smith (in MJ193) crash-landed on 13 June and No 401 Sqn's Flt Lt R R Bouskill (in NH413) force-landed at an ALG when he ran out of fuel. Just to prove that such accidents could befall both novice and veteran alike, Smith (already an ace from his time on Malta in 1942) and Bouskill would claim 12.25 victories between them in coming months.

No 412 Sqn suffered the wing's next fatality when WO L W Love (in MJ384) fell victim to III./JG 2 during an early morning beach patrol north of Troarn. The following day the Spitfires of No 126 Wing began flying into B4 at Bény-sur-Mer, from where they would operate on a permanent basis until 8 August. Future ace Flg Off P M Charron's Spitfire (MJ148) proved to be the day's only casualty, being badly damaged in a landing accident at B4 at 2230 hrs.

Life at the new base for pilots and groundcrew alike was an extremely dusty affair. Whenever a Spitfire took off a huge cloud of choking dust would swirl up and cover just about everything. The dust was so bad that RCAF blue uniforms soon resembled the dull field grey of the German infantry. A warning was posted in the Intelligence

Flt Lt H G Garwood's No 412 Sqn Spitfire MJ255 suffered an engine failure on 11 June, forcing him down near Tilly-sur-Suelles. The aircraft suffered minimal damage in the crash-landing, but it was subsequently written off by passing Allied tanks (these are Canadian Shermans) and vehicles, as this photograph clearly shows. Garwood returned to his unit on 12 June (*Author's Collection*)

Pilots from No 401 Sqn pass the time talking with some of the local inhabitants at B3 Ste Croix-sur-Mer while their Spitfires receive attention. This strip was for Refuelling and Rearming only, temporary sites such as this one allowing the wing to fly more missions during the day prior to returning to RAF Tangmere in the evening (*Public Archives of Canada Pl 30264*)

Air mobility came at a price. Here, the men of No 126 Wing eat lunch outside the mess tent at B4 Bény-sur-Mer in June 1944. European weather, which was often damp, cold and wet, made living in tents an arduous affair for all involved (*Author's Collection via Brian Jeffery Street*)

Two No 126 Wing Intelligence Officers update the situation map on 23 June 1944. Note the warning on the left side of the board telling personnel not to wear their blue uniforms near American lines, and the humorous take on the S.H.A.E.F. acronym (Supreme Headquarters Allied Expeditionary Force) (*DND PL 46076*)

Operations van to remind personnel 'not to go near American lines', as they risked being shot! Life on the continent also came with a whole host of medical problems. Most of the afflictions encountered were boils, scabies, dysentery and VD. In an effort to prevent the pilots from being grounded when suffering from dysentery, many were sustained on a mixture of chalk and opium.

No 401 Sqn lost its first pilot in almost three weeks during the evening of 22 June when 5.5-kill ace Flg Off H E Fenwick (in NH207) was shot down in error by Allied anti-aircraft (AA) fire while chasing a lone German raider near Bayeux. He had claimed all of his kills serving with No 81 Sqn in North Africa in 1942-43.

Few aerial victories came No 126 Wing's way in the final two weeks of June, so the squadrons switched to their secondary role as fighter-bomber and began attacking ground targets in earnest. By the end of June they were dropping bombs (single 500 'pounders') on special targets, shooting up road and rail traffic and generally causing havoc behind enemy lines.

Finally, on 25 June, just as the new British offensive *Epsom* opened up to the west of Caen, No 126 Wing scored in the air again. At 0430 hrs Wg Cdr George Keefer was scrambled, and he quickly shot down a Bf 110 south of Caen – almost certainly a nightfighter on its way home. Keefer's seventh victory would be the only kill claimed that day by either the 2nd TAF or the RAF. While few Luftwaffe aircraft were

seen over the *Epsom* battlefield, USAAF units further west had had a field day, claiming 49 enemy fighters shot down.

For the next two days poor weather greatly restricted 2nd TAF's ability to support *Epsom*, but when conditions improved slightly on 27 June a large number of patrols were launched. At 1255 hrs Spitfires from No 411 Sqn undertook an armed reconnaissance and ran into 15 Fw 190s south of Caen. Sqn Ldr G D Robertson (in MK885) was credited with one

shot down, and three more were claimed as damaged. In return, Flg Off P Wallace (in MK776) bailed out after being shot down by a German fighter. He was returned to B4 that same day. Three hours later at 1525 hrs, Spitfires from No 401 Sqn were scrambled to intercept 12-15 Bf 109s detected in the Beaumont area. Wg Cdr Keefer (in MK826) again led the way, claiming the only kill of the engagement. Enemy flak was particularly heavy, and 12 Spitfires suffered slight damage. Finally, during No 411 Sqn's second patrol of the day, Flt Lt H J Nixon (in MJ857) was shot down by flak at 1700 hrs south of Bayeux. He successfully evaded and eventually returned to the UK in September.

As the *Epsom* offensive struggled forward, the Luftwaffe switched its attention to the British front on 28 June, which in turn meant more action for 2nd TAF's fighter units. That day, while USAAF fighter pilots saw very few enemy aircraft over the American sector and claimed only three shot down, their 2nd TAF counterparts flying Spitfires were credited with 26 kills. It would be their best haul yet, and all of the claims were made by the Canadian units of No 83 Group.

No 412 Sqn opened the scoring at 0615 hrs when future ace Flg Off W J Banks (in NH182) downed a Bf 109 from a formation of six that were intercepted near Bernay – this was the first of his nine kills. At 0910 hrs four No 401 Spitfires set off on patrol, and a short while later they intercepted 20 Fw 190s with a top cover of 20 Bf 109s. In the brief battle that ensued, Flt Lts A F Halcrow (in MJ231) and R M Stayner (in NH260) each claimed a Focke-Wulf fighter destroyed. At 1225 hrs No 411 Sqn took off on the first of three patrols that it would fly during the course of the day. Fifty minutes later, south of Caen, the unit engaged 15 Bf 109s and Fw 190s. Flg Off T R Wheler (in MK885) claimed one Fw 190 destroyed and one damaged, while future ace Flt Lt H C Trainor (in MK311) got a Bf 109 for the first of his 8.5 victories.

At 1920 hrs No 411 Sqn commenced its final patrol of the day, and south of Caen up to 15 Fw 190s and Bf 109s were engaged. Future ace Flt Lt R K Hayward (in MK832) claimed two Fw 190s, having damaged one during the unit's first patrol, while fellow future aces Flt Lts G W Johnson (in MJ474) and H C Trainor (again in MK311) also destroyed an Fw 190 apiece.

No 126 Wing's wing commander flying from April through to 7 July 1944 was Wg Cdr George Keefer, and he flew this Spitfire IX (MK826/ GG-K) for much of that time. He claimed four victories with the aircraft in June 1944, and these combined with his four kills from North Africa in 1941-42 to give Keefer ace status. In November 1944 he was given command of No 125 Wing, equipped with Spitfire XIVs, and he claimed a further four victories with the aircraft through to war's end. Keefer's final tally was 12 destroyed, 2 probables, 9 damaged and 5 destroyed on the ground (*DND PL 31002*)

No 412 Sqn Spitfire VZ-Z sits idle between missions at its new base of B4 Bény-sur-Mer soon after D-Day. Parked behind it is a Typhoon I that appears to have landed at the airfield after suffering engine trouble (*DND PL 30268*)

Finally, at 2115 hrs No 401 Sqn took off for an armed reconnaissance, and while searching for some vehicles to strafe south of Caen the squadron was bounced by a dozen Fw 190s from I./JG 1 and I./JG 11. A fierce dogfight ensued, and future ace Flg Off Bill Klersy (in MK590) claimed two destroyed. Veteran ace Flt Lt I F 'Hap' Kennedy (in NH260) also downed a fighter, recounting the action in his autobiography *Black Crosses off my Wingtip*, published in 1994;

'In the evening, it was "A" flight's turn to patrol. I was "Barley Blue 3". About 40 miles south of Caen at 7000 ft we were looking for German transport moving up to the front. As we were flying on an easterly course, the sun was behind us – always dangerous. Suddenly, I saw a half-dozen Fw 190s coming in quickly out of the sun on our starboard rear quarter, with more up higher behind them.

'"Barley squadron break right! 190s coming down!", I called, and immediately there was a great melee of two-dozen aircraft twisting and turning and firing – a real old fashioned scrap down to ground level. I was somewhat surprised that the FWs didn't dive through at high speed as usual, but a number of them, at least, stayed to fight.

'My new Spit IX was too much for one Focke-Wulf pilot, for although he had a good aircraft, it could not turn with a Spit IX. After two or three hard descending steep turns to the right, I managed to latch onto his tail, but he dove steeply out to the east. I knew I had him, and gave chase at full throttle to ground level. Quickly catching him up, I fired one short burst at 300 yards with both cannon and machine guns and the FW crashed into the trees in a great ball of fire. Flg Lt R Bouskill, "Barley Blue 4", who had remained with me throughout the chase, confirmed this action.'

Flt Lt W R Tew (in MJ231) also destroyed an Fw 190, but both Flt Lt G B Murray and Flt Sgt R B Davidson (in MJ428) were shot down and killed during the clash.

Overall, the three Spitfire wings had claimed 26 victories for the loss of four aircraft and three pilots. No 126 Wing came out on top with 13 victories for the day.

No 411 Sqn's Flt Lt Hugh Trainor (in NH341) got his third kill in 48 hours on 29 June when he downed a Bf 109 five miles west of Caen for the wing's sole victory of the day. Trainor (again in NH341) claimed another Messerschmitt fighter destroyed the following day too when he was one of three No 126 Wing pilots to be credited with victories. The first kill came at 1440 hrs when No 401 Sqn intercepted 12 Fw 190s and Bf 109s north of Caen during an armed reconnaissance over the Argentan-Falaise area. Flt Lt R M Stayner (in NH260) destroyed a Bf 109, but the unit in turn had Flg Off D D Ashleigh (in MH872) shot down by flak. He force-landed near Mormal and returned to base on foot.

A short while later No 411 Sqn took off to dive-bomb the Bretteville crossroads, but they were bounced by six Fw 190s near Caen and forced to jettison their bombs. Unit CO Sqn Ldr Graham Robertson (in MJ474) quickly turned the tables and shot down one his attackers. Finally, during the last patrol of the day, which commenced at 2030 hrs, Flt Lt Hugh Trainor got a Bf 109 over Thury Hurcourt. This was the 22nd, and last, victory claimed by No 83 Group's Spitfire units on 30 June 1944.

When all the numbers were added up, No 126 Wing had had an impressive month. Its Spitfires had logged more than 3000 hours in the air whilst flying a total of 1648 operational sorties. The wing's scoreboard for June stood at 28 enemy aircraft destroyed, one probable and 11 damaged.

By the end of the month the Allies had been able to construct nine ALGs in the British sector, some of which were still coming under German shellfire, and 11 in the US zone. In total, the Allies had landed 875,000 troops. On a less positive note, 30 June also saw the suspension of Operation *Epsom* following a robust German counterattack.

NEW MONTH, MORE ACTION

By 1 July conditions at B4 had drastically improved, as had base security. Surprisingly, despite some of the world's largest land battles raging all around them, personnel of No 126 Wing were now being given half-days off. Some went sightseeing while others travelled to the nearby town of Bayeux to relax. The food situation had improved greatly too, with quantities of French wine, Calvados and eggs also pouring in to supplement standard rations.

Flt Lt Trainor (in MK423) did his best to keep up his amazing scoring run on the 1st, but this time he could only claim a Bf 109 as a probable. Three more Messerschmitts were credited to Nos 411 and 401 Sqns during separate skirmishes east of Caen, and Flg Off G D Billings (in ML135) crash-landed south of Carentan after being hit by flak. He successfully evaded.

2 July proved to be a very productive day for No 126 Wing, and it began early when No 411 Sqn took off on patrol at 0550 hrs. Forty minutes later four Fw 190s from II./JG 26 were spotted southwest of Caen and one was shot down by Flt Lt E G Lapp (in NH196) for the loss of WO J S Jeffrey (in NH341). The latter bailed out and evaded capture, rejoining his unit the following month.

At 1130 hrs Spitfires of No 412 Sqn took to the air to escort No 122 Wing Mustangs over the Lisieux area. Some 45 minutes into the mission at least ten German fighters were spotted and engaged, with four Fw 190s being quickly shot down. Two were credited to future ace Flt Lt Don Laubman (in MJ485), while Sqn Ldr J E Sheppard (in MJ304) claimed one for his fifth, and last, kill. Future ace Plt Off D R C Jamieson (in NH346) also claimed his first victory. Sadly, Flg Off H W Bowker (in MK199) was last seen diving away into cloud with an Fw 190 glued to his tail. Bowker, who had four victories and

Being a mobile wing meant most, if not all, maintenance and assorted tasks had to be done outdoors. Here, the vital job of parachute packing is done on the ground early in the Normandy campaign (*Public Archives of Canada PL 31784*)

a probable to his name, was later confirmed as having been killed.

At 1550 hrs No 401 Sqn clashed with 24 Fw 190s and Bf 109s during a sweep east of Caen. Two Bf 109s were destroyed, one of which gave Flg Off Bill Klersy (in MK590) ace status. The second victory was claimed by Flt Lt 'Hap' Kennedy (in NH247), taking his final tally to ten and five shared destroyed and one probable. Most of these had come flying Spitfires over the Mediterranean and Italy in 1943. Kennedy would become CO of No 401 Sqn three days later.

By dusk on 2 July 2nd TAF Spitfire pilots had claimed 25 destroyed, three probables and 27 damaged. Flg Off Bowker had been the day's solitary casualty.

During the battle of Normandy, and for all of northwest Europe for that matter, German flak was both effective and frequently deadly. On 3 July, for example, it claimed No 401 Sqn CO Sqn Ldr L M Cameron. His Spitfire (MJ131) was hit while attacking motor transport and he crash-landed north of Falaise. Initially managing to evade capture, Cameron was eventually caught, but he succeeded in escaping from his captors and was duly back in action by September.

As the Allied advance began to slow to a crawl due to the heavy resistance it was encountering on the ground, German fighter units were more active than ever in support of the Wehrmacht. Indeed, on 4 July they mounted 522 sorties. With so much activity, it was inevitable that No 126 Wing would get the chance to add to its growing score of aerial victories, and at 1820 hrs No 411 Sqn engaged a mixed formation of Fw 190s and Bf 109s southeast of Caen. Seizing his chance to 'make ace', Flt Lt Hugh Trainor (in MJ994) claimed two Bf 109s shot down. Flt Lt Bob Hayward (in MK382) also passed the

Flg Off H W 'Bud' Bowker of No 411 Sqn checks his guns at B3 Ste Croix-sur-Mer – note the German helmet covering the cannon muzzle. Having served with No 412 Sqn throughout 1943, and claimed two victories and one probable in the air and one destroyed and one damaged on the ground during this time, Bowker was posted to No 410 Repair and Servicing Unit for a rest. Yet despite being with a support unit he still managed to claim two Fw 190s destroyed on 22 May 1944. Returning to No 412 Sqn the following month, Bowker looked destined to 'make ace', but on 2 July 1944 he was killed dogfighting with an Fw 190 near Lisieux (*DND PL 30259*)

GERMAN FLAK DEFENCES

The Luftwaffe had the responsibility of controlling German flak defences. The units tasked with this mission were both well armed and well trained, and during the battle of Normandy they provided the Germans with the most effective means by which to defend themselves against the marauding fighter-bombers. They could also be used in ground defence.

When the Allies landed, the Luftwaffe soon called in reinforcements. To help counter the tactical and strategic air effort against German forces, the Luftwaffe transferred a total of 140 heavy and 50 light flak batteries into France.

By the time the Allies reached the Rhine the need for the Germans to protect transportation routes, including railway lines and waterways, had become critical – so much so that flak defences from industrial targets were repositioned alongside roads, train tracks and waterways. In November 1944 the Luftwaffe transferred 500 heavy and light flak guns to the protection of transportation routes. Indeed, the Luftwaffe established a 'flak belt' along the entire course of the River Rhine in order to protect shipping.

The most effective weapon used by the Germans was the excellent four-barrelled Flakviering 38. Its four 20 mm cannon proved deadly against low-

flying aircraft. Unfortunately for pilots flying the Spitfire, their aircraft was extremely vulnerable to ground fire. A single hole in the chin-mounted oil tank, damage to the underwing radiators or a glycol pipe fracture could end a flight in a hurry – none of these components were armoured. For the pilots of No 126 Wing, German flak defences would prove their deadliest foe.

It is also pertinent to note that many Allied aircraft were shot down by so-called friendly fire. Aircraft recognition was not a strong suit for Allied gunners, either ashore or at sea. The following communication from Air Officer Commanding No 11 Group, AVM H W L Saunders (a 15-kill SE 5a ace from World War 1), dated 12 June 1944, sheds some light on the problem;

'I have been impressed in the past week with the excellent work of all squadrons in the air, on many occasions under very difficult weather conditions, and I wish to congratulate all concerned. I wish all pilots to know that everything possible is being done to reduce to a minimum AA fire from friendly shipping and the beach area. The navy and army are eulogistic regarding the fighter cover provided, and I know full well will do their best to avoid unfortunate incidents.'

Above left
A Flakvierling 38 anti-aircraft gun mounted on a SdKfz 7/1 half-track. The four-barrelled Flak 38 was an extremely effective weapon against low-flying Allied fighter-bombers. The 20 mm cannon had a maximum horizontal range of 5320 yards and a maximum vertical range of 12,500 ft. However, rounds from the Flak 38 did not normally reach this altitude because the weapon typically fired

six-second self-destroying tracer ammunition. With a rate of fire of 1400 rounds per minute and an effective ceiling of 7218 ft, the Flak 38 made dive-bombing or strafing a hazardous affair. Most losses suffered by the 2nd TAF were due to 20 mm and 37 mm anti-aircraft guns (*ww2images.com*)

Above right
Anti-aircraft fire over the Normandy

beachhead. Many Allied fighters fell victim to friendly anti-aircraft fire – D-Day stripes alone were not foolproof. Unfortunately, there were also far too many accounts, both official and personal, of Allied units being bombed or strafed by friendly aircraft. Some have estimated that literally thousands of Allied troops were killed and wounded by the RAF and USAAF (*Public Archives of Canada PA 138754*)

Recently promoted Sqn Ldr Bob Hayward poses in the cockpit of his Spitfire IX *CALAMITY JANE, VI.* (serial unknown) sometime after becoming CO of No 411 Sqn in August 1944. One of a number of ex-RCAF flying instructors to serve with No 126 Wing, Hayward commenced combat operations with No 401 Sqn in March 1943. Having claimed two and one shared kills, one shared probable and one shared damaged with this unit, he joined No 411 Sqn as a flight commander in May 1944. Promoted to CO on 5 August, Hayward had scored a further three kills and four damaged by the time his tour ended in September 1944 (*Public Archives of Canada PMR 78-251*)

magical five-victory mark when he downed an Fw 190. Late in the day a 'bogey' was reported near Falaise, and at 2200 hrs No 411 Sqn scrambled Sqn Ldr G D Robertson (in MK885) and Flt Lt Trainor (in MK423) to investigate. They duly shared in the destruction of a Do 217 northeast of Cabourg.

On 5 July No 126 Wing claimed two Fw 190s shot down when Nos 401 and 412 Sqns intercepted four German fighters at low-level near Chartres at noon. One was claimed by Flg Off Laubman (in MJ485) of No 412 Sqn and the second fell to future ace Flg Off R M Davenport (in ML142) of No 401 Sqn – this was his first victory.

Forty-eight hours later No 126 Wing again found itself in the thick of the action, with fierce engagements being fought across the invasion area. The first took place at 0710 hrs when Spitfires from No 412 Sqn clashed with German fighters attacking RAF Mustangs near Bernay. Flg Off W J Banks (in NH182) claimed a Bf 109 destroyed for his second of nine victories, and fellow future ace Plt Off D R C Jamieson downed an Fw 190 for his second of eight kills.

Soon after 1100 hrs Spitfires from No 401 Sqn tangled with 12+ Bf 109s near Cabourg, and one was shot down by Flt Lt W R McRae (in MK560). Minutes later No 401 Sqn engaged four Bf 109s and 20 Fw 190s near Lisieux, and Flt Lt A L Sinclair (in MK579) claimed one of each destroyed – he noted in his combat report that the Bf 109 dove into the ground before he could actually open fire.

No 412 Sqn was back in the air at 1420 hrs, patrolling over Bernay, L'Aigle and Argentan. German fighters were again encountered and two Fw 190s claimed shot down. One was credited to Flt Lt R I A Smith (in ML113) for his seventh kill – this was his first victory since 25 October 1942. The second fell to Flg Off G T Schwalm (in NH212). Flt Lt W B Needham (in MK622) fell to flak southwest of Falaise a short while later, the pilot evading and returning to B4.

At 1630 hrs it was No 411 Sqn's turn to mount an armed reconnaissance, and its pilots found eight to ten Fw 190s east of Caen. One was shot down by Flt Lt G W Johnson (in MJ474) for his third of eight kills. In the final action of the day, No 401 Sqn pilots reported engaging at least eight Bf 109s near Falaise, and Flt Lt Tew (in MJ231) was credited with destroying one of them. This brought No 126 Wing's victory tally for 7 July to nine destroyed. It was a fitting send off for Wg Cdr George Keefer, who was declared tour expired on this date and replaced as wing leader by fellow ace Sqn Ldr B D 'Dal' Russel from No 442 Sqn. This was Russel's second posting to the unit as Wing Commander Flying, as he had briefly held the post as a supernumerary in the spring of 1943.

It is interesting to note that at this time two communiqués were issued to the Spitfire wings. While the latter had been successfully flying armed reconnaissance and patrols since D-Day, the powers that be realised that their tactics would have to change going forward. The first one was issued by No 17 (F) Sector HQ, RCAF to the wing commanders of Nos 126, 127 and 144 Wings on 7 July 1944;

'When flak and weather conditions permit, armed recces are to be carried out between 3000-5000 ft so that a maximum of ground movement may be observed, as that is the prime objective of an armed recce. This is naturally left to your discretions and judgment entirely, but I wish you to keep this in mind, and instruct all squadron and section leaders to do the same.

'It is particularly important that we do not have reports going forward to Group which indicate that armed recces are being done at any height up to 20,000-25,000 ft. Please bring this to the attention of all reporting officers.'

The second communiqué was issued to the same wings by No 17 (F) Sector HQ, RCAF on 10 July, and it seems to address the issue of the Spitfire's weak gun armament. Parts of it read as follows;

'With regard to the policy of fighter aircraft carrying out armed reconnaissance of roads aimed at the destruction of the enemy's lines of communication, it is considered that maximum effort is not being obtained by the present method.

'Therefore, it has been decided that in the future, where conditions permit, a portion of the force involved will carry bombs. The target for the bombs will be a target of opportunity decided by the leader of the formation. In the event of no such target(s) presenting itself, the leader will instruct pilots to attack a "last resort" target selected with the aid of the Army Liaison Coordinator during the briefing.

'It is emphasised that accurately placed bombs in such positions as crossroads and at the head of suspected convoy movements will prove of great value.

'It is suggested that in a formation of three to four aircraft, at least two of them carry bombs, and in a formation of two to six, all of them should carry bombs.

'The further aim in view is to keep the pilots in constant practice with the technique of bombing, and to develop this technique in new pilots.

'Squadrons will be advised by Sector Ops when to bomb up, and under no circumstances are pilots to return with bombs. They must be dropped well inside enemy lines.

'Bombing heights are to be left to the discretion of the leader of the formation. However, it is suggested that at least a 5000-6000 ft ceiling

Sqn Ldr Bob Hayward strikes a typical fighter pilot's pose in this official photograph taken in the late summer of 1944. He received the DSO and DFC for his exploits with No 126 Wing, thus becoming the only No 411 Sqn CO to earn both decorations (*DND PL 28539*)

should be available in order to maintain the accuracy required for effective dive-bombing.'

What is both surprising and revealing about these two communiqués is the amount of discretion formation leaders had when it came to target selection and tactics. One might have also assumed that dive-bombing techniques would have been well developed and put into practice long before the invasion had taken place.

Operational flying in a combat zone had an intensity all of its own. Aircraft flew four or five times a day, which meant that they had to be rearmed and refuelled quickly (another drawback of the Spitfire's modest fuel capacity was that the fighter's tanks had to be constantly topped up between missions). The hectic pace meant quick meals or no food at all for both pilots and groundcrew. And with the short evenings during the height of the summer, there was very little time for sleep.

The onset of morning mists greatly reduced operational flying over Normandy from the second week of July, and this meant that No 126 Wing had to wait until the early evening of the 12th to score its next aerial victory. Flg Off W J Banks (in MJ959) claimed his third kill when he destroyed one of two Bf 109s spotted by a quartet of No 412 Sqn Spitfires near Mortagne. He and his squadronmates had been on their way to bomb a railway bridge at Le Mesnil at the time.

On 14 July an organisational change was made in the make-up of several wings. No 144 Wing was broken up, with No 441 'Silver Fox' Sqn moving to No 125 Wing, No 443 'Hornet' Sqn to No 127 Wing and No 442 'Caribou' Sqn joining No 126 Wing. The expansion of the latter wing also necessitated a change in command, with Wg Cdr Keith Hodson, who had led the unit through the difficult days of 1943 as well as the D-Day invasion, being replaced by Grp Capt G E McGregor. An excellent pilot and capable administrator, McGregor had 'made ace' during the Battle of Britain, earning him one of the first Distinguished Flying Crosses to be awarded to a Canadian pilot in World War 2.

No 126 Wing added four more kills to its tally that same day. The first fell to No 411 Sqn at 1430 hrs during beach patrols in the Lisieux area, Flg Offs T R Wheler (in NH317) and J N Harrison (in MJ468) each downing an Fw 190 northwest of Caen. At 2000 hrs four Spitfires from No 401 Sqn encountered a large number of German fighters over Bayeux, and Flg Offs T P Jarvis (in ML118) and C P B Wyman (in MK590) destroyed a Bf 109 apiece.

No 126 Wing scored the first kill of the day on 15 July when four aircraft from No 412 Sqn engaged 30+ Fw 190s of I. and III./JG 26 southeast of Caen. Despite being outnumbered, Flg Off L F Berryman (in MJ772) claimed the first of his four kills during the clash. At 2125 hours the wing suffered its first loss in more than a week when No 411 Sqn's Flt Lt D H Evans (in MK462) bailed out northeast of Caen after being hit by flak. He successfully evaded. A second Spitfire was also damaged at the same time, although its pilot managed to return to B4.

Forty-eight hours later No 411 Sqn again met the enemy in the air, although on this occasion the opposition consisted of just a solitary Bf 109 northeast of Lisieux. Sqn Ldr G D Robertson (in MK885) made short work of it, attaining ace status in the process. At 2220 hrs

A group photograph of No 442 Sqn in Normandy shortly after D-Day. The unit's CO, Sqn Ldr Harry Dowding, is the pilot casually leaning on the bottom right propeller blade. Along with Nos 441 and 430 Sqns, No 442 Sqn was one of the first units to operate from French soil. It would join No 126 Wing from No 144 Wing in mid-July 1944 (*Public Archives of Canada PMR 79-631*)

Flg Off Charles Fox of No 412 Sqn poses for the camera. He was just one of a number of pilots from three units (Nos 412, 193 and 602 Sqn) who claimed credit for the strafing and wounding of the 'Desert Fox', Generalfeldmarschall Erwin Rommel, on 17 July 1944. No 126 Wing's Summary of Operations for that date does not mention a 'staff car' being shot at or damaged by Spitfires of No 412 Sqn, however. The proof available is not conclusive as to who actually attacked Rommel. Aside from his strafing exploits, Fox was also credited with shooting down four German aircraft and damaging five others (*DND 28275*)

that evening, Flt Lt W T Klersy (in MK362) and Flg Off R M Davenport (in ML142) downed two of three Do 217s that were intercepted by No 401 Sqn over the Caen-Cabourg-Le Havre area. The third bomber escaped with damage.

On 18 July British and Canadian forces launched Operation *Goodwood* in an attempt to complete the encirclement of Caen, while US forces were in the final stages of their preparation for the long awaited breakout in the south seven days later, codenamed Operation *Cobra*. Poor weather coincided with the start of these offensives, and No 126 Wing's mission tally was adversely affected as a result for more than a week. After several days of flying without results (MJ364 was written off in a crash-landing at B4 due to engine failure on 18 July, however), the pilots of No 442 Sqn at last got the chance to show their prowess at 1315 hrs on 20 July when a flight of four Spitfires attacked 40+ Fw 190s from JG 1 southeast of St Lô. Three German fighters

were downed, two by Flt Lt W A Olmsted (in MJ520) and one by Flg Off G R Blair (no serial recorded). This action was recorded in No 126 Wing Summary of Operations No 27 as follows;

'The next patrol climbed to high altitude at 20,000-25,000 ft between Bayeux and a point ten miles north of Cabourg. It was carried out by No 442 Sqn, with four aircraft taking off at 1227 hrs and landing at 1434 hrs. When south of Caen they were warned of a large number of bogeys, and shortly thereafter ran into about 40+ Fw 190s over St Lô at 23,000 ft. In the ensuing battle Flt Lt W A Olmsted destroyed two Fw 190s and Flg Off C R Blair destroyed one Fw 190. Of the two aircraft shot down by Flt Lt Olmsted, one burst into flames and the other exploded violently in mid-air, much flying debris hitting Flt Lt Olmsted's aircraft. The pilot of Flg Off Blair's destroyed was seen to bail out after Flg Off Blair had expended all his ammo.'

What is remarkable about the above description is the fearlessness shown by the pilots of No 126 Wing. Outnumbered at least ten-to-one, they did not hesitate to attack. This engagement clearly illustrates that the single most important quality needed by a fighter pilot was aggressiveness. The other critical point is that in order to get close enough to shoot down an aircraft, one had to expose oneself to a counter blow. The pilots who knew this and accepted the dangerous reality had the advantage. Add in excellent training, a high degree of skill, leadership and good luck, and the chances of a pilot scoring a victory increased considerably.

Fifteen minutes after this action, elements from No 401 Sqn would add two more Fw 190s to No 126 Wing's ever increasing tally after they were vectored to the fight involving Olmsted and Blair. Flt Lts R M Stayner (in NH260) and A F Halcrow (in ML306) each destroyed a fighter, the former claiming his third, and final, kill. These victories also brought No 401 Sqn's tally to exactly 100, the first 29 of these having been claimed in 1940 when the unit was designated No 1 Sqn RCAF. The day's final success went to No 412 Sqn's Plt Off D R C Jamieson (in NH346), who claimed an Fw 190 destroyed south of La Hogue for his fourth kill.

A pair of No 442 Sqn Spitfires take off for another sortie over Normandy. Both carry 44-gallon drop tanks on their centreline racks. Because of the Spitfire's poor endurance (it had the shortest range of all the Allied single-seat fighters), drop tanks were a must. Originally designed for the Hurricane, these tanks gave the Spitfire the ability to fly to the German border. They also extended the fighter's patrol time over the invasion beaches. During the early stages of the Normandy landings nine fighter squadrons (six of them equipped with Spitfires) were assigned to patrol the beaches during daylight hours (*Author's Collection*)

For the next three days more bad weather would limit the wing to just 48 sorties.

At 1530 hrs on 24 July four pilots from No 412 Sqn would again take on 40+ Bf 109s and Fw 190s east of Lisieux and emerge with seven victories to their credit. Leading the way was Flg Off W J Banks (in MJ485), who 'made ace' in style by downing two Bf 109s and an Fw 190 – these victories also pushed No 126 Wing's score past the 100 mark since its inception. Plt Off D R C Jamieson (in NH346) followed suit with a pair of Bf 109s, while Flt Lt O M Linton (in MJ147) claimed two Fw 190s. The latter had previously scored 1.5 kills and two and five shared damaged with No 249 Sqn during the defence of Malta in 1942. On a less positive note, Flt Lt W R Tew (in MJ231) fell victim to flak over Lisieux during an armed reconnaissance. He bailed out and successfully evaded.

Flak also claimed No 401 Sqn CO Sqn Ldr 'Hap' Kennedy (in MK311) at 1550 hrs on 26 July during a sweep near the airfield at Dreux. He 'was forced to bail out southwest of Creton, and was seen to land safely'. Kennedy evaded and returned to Allied lines (but not to No 126 Wing) on 24 August. His place at No 401 Sqn was taken by fellow ace Sqn Ldr Hugh Trainor.

The following day, as if to avenge the loss of their CO, the pilots of No 401 Sqn enjoyed their best day of the war to date in terms of aerial victories when they claimed nine enemy fighters during 45 sorties. The No 126 Wing Summary of Operations No 34 described the first action of a memorable day for the unit;

'Sqn Ldr H C Trainor (in MK590) led 12 aircraft from No 401 Sqn on his first mission as CO with excellent results. The squadron was airborne at 0627 hrs on an Armed Recce covering the Falaise area. They encountered 40+ '109s and '190s flying west at 15,000 ft in the area southwest of Caen. A combat ensued, resulting in the destruction of seven Me 109s and one Fw 190 and the damaging of one Me 109. In three instances the pilots of the enemy aircraft bailed out.

'Flg Off G A Bell (in MK300) claims the destruction of one enemy aircraft without firing his guns. He chased a '109 starting from 15,000 ft down to 5000 ft, and during this period it spun on three occasions. At 5000 ft Bell was still following when the '109 turned to starboard, flicked over and spun into the deck. Flt Lt A E Morrison (in PL280) claims one Fw 190. One Me 109 each were destroyed by the following – Sqn Ldr Trainor, Flt Lt G W Johnson (in ML264), Flt Lt A F Halcrow (in NH260), Flg Off M H Havers (in MK632), Flt Lt W R McRae (in MJ951) and Flg Off C P B Wyman (in NH247), who also damaged one. The squadron pancaked at 0748 hrs.'

Flg Off Wilf Banks (on the right) is given a 'fist full of francs' for bagging the 100th German aircraft destroyed by No 126 Wing since its inception. He accomplished the feat on 24 July 1944 when he downed two Bf 109s and an Fw 190 east of Lisieux. These kills gave Banks ace status, and by the time he left No 412 Sqn in early March 1945 his tally stood at nine destroyed, three probables and one damaged (*Public Archives of Canada PL 30911*)

At 1600 hrs three of No 411 Sqn's Spitfires were hit by flak east of Fleury-sur-Andelle and Flt Lt H J Nixon (in NH344) force-landed. He successfully evaded. No 401 Sqn's final victory came at 1910 hrs when Flt Lt R R Bouskill (in ML305) claimed an Fw 190 southeast of Caen for the first of his five kills.

No 411 Sqn suffered yet another loss to flak at 1005 hrs on 30 July when Flg Off H W Kramer (in ML295) crash-landed near Fauguernon. He too evaded.

Having enjoyed such success during July, it was fitting that No 401 Sqn should claim the final two victories of the month, although they came at a price. Having been grounded in the morning by thick fog, 12 Spitfires from the unit took off on an armed reconnaissance at 1220 hrs and headed for the Lisieux-Domfront area. A similar number of Fw 190s from II./JG 1 were encountered near Domfront, and aces Sqn Ldr Trainor (in NH260) and Flt Lt Klersy (in MK590) each destroyed a German fighter. However, Flt Lt T P Jarvis (in MJ662) was killed when he too was shot down in the same engagement.

July had been No 126 Wing's best month to date in terms of aerial victories. Some 56 enemy aircraft had been destroyed (the vast majority were single-seat fighters) during the course of 3429 sorties. These successes meant that in June/July, the wing had amassed a score of 89 enemy aircraft shot down. The Spitfire units' ground attack statistics during the same period were even more impressive, No 126 Wing having dropped 121 500-lb bombs and listed 242 mechanised transports as 'flamers', 31 as 'smokers' and 297 damaged.

AUGUST ACTION

The beginning of August would see the Allied armies on the move at last. Since D-Day their advance from the beachhead had been a slow and arduous task. Determined German resistance, the bocage terrain, supply problems and weather had all conspired against the Allies, but on 25 July Operation *Cobra* opened a gap south of St Lô in the American sector. This had been achieved because British and Canadians forces had managed to hold the bulk of the German armour (seven panzer divisions, four of which were SS) between Caumont and Caen in an operation codenamed *Bluecoat*. The latter was specifically devised to aid US forces assigned to *Cobra*, who now faced just two Panzer divisions with a total of 150 tanks. By 1 August the US First Army had broken out of the beachhead and was pouring south towards Loire and Brittany.

No 126 Wing's operational tempo remained high, with air patrols, armed reconnaissance and dive-bombing sorties being continuously generated throughout the hours of daylight.

The new month started badly for No 442 Sqn when Flg Off W R Campbell (in MK826) was shot down and killed by flak southwest of Argences. Although he was seen to bail out of his fighter, Campbell did not survive the incident. The first claim for August came the following afternoon when Flg Off T M Saunderson (in NH182) of No 412 Sqn destroyed an Fw 190 during a scrap with 22 German fighters west of Ecouches. Tempering this success was the loss of his CO, Sqn Ldr Sheppard (in MJ304), who was shot down by a Bf 109 from I./JG 5 in

Pilots of No 411 Sqn gather round AOC RCAF Overseas Air Marshal L S Breadner at B4 Bény-sur-Mer on 1 August 1944. During World War 2 Breadner turned the RCAF into one of the most powerful air forces in the world. A Royal Naval Air Service fighter pilot in World War 1, he was AOC RCAF from January 1944 to May 1945 (*DND PI 31002*)

the same fight. Although captured, Sheppard escaped and was back in Allied hands by 12 August. He did not rejoin his unit, however, future ace Sqn Ldr Dean Dover having been transferred in from No 442 Sqn to take Sheppard's place.

Shortly after noon on 3 August 12 Spitfires from No 401 Sqn ran into a dozen Bf 109s south of Domfront, three of which were quickly despatched by Flt Lt G W Johnson (in ML305), whose claim made him an ace, Flt Lt R H Cull (serial not recorded) and future ace Flt Lt R R Bouskill (in MK721). A week would pass before No 126 Wing managed its next aerial success. The units were far from idle in the interim, however, as they managed to destroy 38 mechanised transports in the space of just seven days. Spitfire MK941 of No 411 Sqn's Flg Off T R Wheeler was badly hit by flak on one such mission on 7 August, and he bailed out near Lisieux after nursing the aircraft back to Allied-held territory.

The following day all four units in the wing moved southwest to B18 Cristot so as to be nearer to the slowly advancing Allied armies.

On 10 August 12 aircraft from No 412 Sqn left B18 to patrol the area around Alencon. Led by Wg Cdr B D Russel, the unit, which was at 12,000 ft, spotted 12 Bf 109s 5000 ft below them and dove into the attack. Single Bf 109s were destroyed by Flg Offs C R Symons (in MJ292) and D C Laubman (in MH486), with a third fighter being shared between the latter pilot and T M Saunderson (in NH182). The rest of the wing contributed a further 23 mechanised transports destroyed to its burgeoning tally.

The mobile fighter-bomber wing was one of the most versatile and destructive weapons used during World War 2. This was shown to deadly effect on 12 August when No 126 Wing flew 139 sorties in both the air-to-air and air-to-ground roles. The follow excerpts come from No 126 Wing's Summary of Operations No 50, which covered 24 hours of combat from dawn on 12 August;

'Flying started at 0716 hrs when four aircraft of No 442 Sqn were airborne on a weather Recce. They landed at 0847 hrs after having located 8+ enemy tanks and armoured vehicles. One of these tanks was damaged. The "blitz" on the Hun started properly at 1042 hrs when 12 aircraft of No 412 Sqn were airborne to do an Armed Recce in sections covering the side roads between Flers and Argentan. They landed at 1155 hrs with a score of five flamers, four smokers and 18 damaged, as well as one troop carrying vehicle also shot up.

'No 401 Sqn started the afternoon with six aircraft Dive-Bombing a special target at 1336-1405 hrs. Of the six bombs dropped, four burst in the target area, one overshot and one hung up, which was jettisoned in the target area.

No 126 Wing pilots proudly pose with a portion of tailplane from a downed Ju 88 that lists their achievements after a hard day's flying on 12 August 1944. Standing in the back row, from left to right, are Flg Off R M Cook and Flt Lts A F Halcrow and R Hyndman. In the centre row, again from left to right, are Flg Offs H A Crawford and G H Mercer and Flt Lts Ken Robb and E G Lapp. In the front row, from left to right, are Flg Off J M Portz, Flt Lt G W Johnson, Sqn Ldr H C Trainor, Flg Off B Eskow and Flt Lt A M Tooley (*DND PL 31347*)

'Nos 411 and 412 Sqns both went on a Sweep with 12 aircraft each at 1744-1910 hrs. No 411 Sqn, led by Wg Cdr Russel, ran into four Me 109s and three Fw 190s just east of Alencon, destroying four and damaging one, for no loss. Flg Offs G H Mercer (in NH205), J J Boyle (in MJ468) and H A Crawford (in NH196) and Flt Lt E G Lapp (in NH174) were credited with an Me 109 destroyed each, and Flt Lt A M Tooley (in MJ899) with an Fw 190 damaged.

'No 411 Sqn finished the day with six aircraft Dive-Bombing a road on the outskirts of Falaise. Visibility was very bad due to haze, and only near misses were scored.

'At the end of the day the totals for No 126 Wing were as follows – four enemy aircraft destroyed, 23 mechanised transports, one troop carrying vehicle, one armoured fighting vehicle and one tank damaged. A total of 18 500-lb bombs were dropped.'

The only casualty of this busy day was No 412 Sqn's Flg Off G T Schwalm (in NH189), who was killed when his Spitfire was shot down at 1450 hrs near Falaise. On 13 August two more Spitfires fell to flak, No 412 Sqn's WO G J Young (in MK576) bailing out southwest of Vassy. He was captured and subsequently executed by the Gestapo 12 days later. No 442 Sqn's Flt Lt W B Randell (in MK141) was appreciably luckier, crash-landing near Camilly and quickly returning to B18. Flg Off R Symons (in MJ350) bailed out of his machine over Allied lines on the 14th after it was hit by flak north of Vimoutiers.

No 401 Sqn's Flt Lt Russ Bouskill (in NH260) claimed his third kill at 1930 hrs on 17 August when his unit engaged 30+ Fw 190s that were attacking Typhoons near Bernay.

BATTLE OF FALAISE

While No 126 Wing continued with its air and ground attacks, the situation on the ground was changing rapidly. On 7 August, desperate to stop the American advance, Hitler had ordered a counterattack to begin just north of Mortain. It lasted just six days and achieved virtually nothing. By 9 August the Allies realised that the German attack could be stalled and pinched off, possibly trapping the entire German force in France. The resulting battle would become known as the Battle of Falaise, and No 126 Wing would play a big part in it. With the Allies pressing the Germans from three sides, the last battle of Normandy was about to begin.

The battle for the Falaise Pocket was fought from 8 to 23 August. When the Wehrmacht's fighting retreat turned into a rout, it was pummelled from the air with devastating results. As the air attacks intensified the shrinking pocket become known to the attackers as 'The Shambles' (an old English term for a slaughterhouse). The battle reached its peak on 18 August, and No 126 Wing's summary of operations for that day began on an optimistic note;

'Another fine day set the wing off to an early start. Operations which started much the same as any others in the past few days soon reached unprecedented heights, and resulted in the highest score of enemy transport yet reached by this wing, and perhaps any other wing.'

By the end of the day the totals were indeed impressive. Some 195 sorties had been flown and 220 mechanised transports destroyed, 151 left smoking and 292 damaged. The wing also claimed four tanks destroyed, five left smoking and 15 damaged, eight armoured fighting vehicles destroyed, two left smoking and six damaged, one ammunition dump destroyed, one troop carrying vehicle destroyed and 70 troops killed.

A high price was paid for this success, however, with No 401 Sqn CO Sqn Ldr Trainor (in NH260) 'last seen flying at 2000 ft'. Hit by flak, he crash-landed near Lisieux and evaded until he returned to his unit on 25 August. Sadly, squadronmate Flg Off C E Fairfield (in MK284) perished when he crashed in flames after being struck by flak too. Two hours later, No 442 Sqn's Flg Offs J P Lumsden (in PL280) and J G Doyle (in MH718) were also brought down by flak, the former bailing out off Cabourg and being rescued and the latter crash-landing at B18. At 1505 hrs Flt Lt A F Halcrow (in MJ899) bailed out of his flak-damaged fighter near Vimoutiers and was captured. He eventually persuaded his guards to let him go, however, when he promised to send back Allied troops to take them prisoner! The wing's final loss of the day was No 401 Sqn's Flg Off R M Davenport (in ML142), who crash-landed in Allied territory.

In total, No 83 Group would claim 1074 vehicles and 73 tanks destroyed during the Battle of Falaise, No 84 Group adding a further 230 vehicles and 37 tanks to the total.

19 August saw the pilots of No 126 Wing back in the air achieving similar results to the previous day – 136 mechanised transports destroyed, 60 left smoking and 186 damaged, six armoured fighting vehicles destroyed and four tanks damaged. This time two German fighters were also downed by No 401 Sqn when 12 of its Spitfires ran into 40+ Fw 190s and Bf 109s east of Bernay. Flt Lt J C Lee (in MK230) got an Fw 190 and ace Flt Lt G W Johnson (in ML305) downed a Bf 109. Flak exacted a heavy toll once again, with No 442 Sqn's Flt Lt D M McDuff (in ML152) bailing out near Bernay. He was initially captured but eventually evaded. No 412 Sqn's Flg Off C R Symons (in MJ844) perished, however, when his fighter was brought down near Vimoutiers.

Late the following day Flg Offs D F Husband (in ML129) and R M Davenport (in ML118) of No 401 Sqn destroyed an Fw 190 each west of Evreux, these successes taking 2nd TAF's Fw 190 destroyed claims to 11 for 20 August.

After the battle the Falaise area was examined by an Operational Research Section of 21st Army Group. In a limited area alone they counted the wreckage of 344 tanks, self-propelled guns and armoured cars, plus 252 towed guns (with their dead horse teams beside them) and close to 2500 trucks and lorries.

No 442 Sqn engine fitters work on a Merlin at B18 Cristot in August 1944. The Spitfire was extremely vulnerable to ground fire and ricochets from its own guns. Seen here in between the two mechanics is the fighter's 5.6 Imp gallon (25 litre) oil tank. If this reservoir was punctured in flight it quickly lost all fluid, causing the engine to seize up and burst into flames. Other vulnerable areas were the glycol tank located just behind the spinner and the oil and coolant radiators under the wings (*DND PL 31362*)

The aftermath of the Battle of Falaise. Allied tactical air power was most effective when the Germans were in full retreat. During the battle for Falaise the Wehrmacht lost thousand of vehicles that were either destroyed by Allied aircraft, abandoned due to a lack of fuel or blown up by their own forces so as to avoid them being captured intact. Despite having invented the concept of *Blitzkrieg*, the Wehrmacht was in fact one of the least mobile armies of World War 2, with the majority of its transports being horse drawn. In these three photographs the shattered remains of artillery pieces, a Sturmgeschutz self-propelled gun, a 75 mm Pak 40 anti-tank gun, a SdKfz 9 halftrack, horse drawn carriages and numerous trucks and smaller vehicles can all be clearly seen. They had fallen victim to strafing attacks by No 126 Wing (*National Archives*)

By 22 August the Wehrmacht in France had effectively ceased to exist – No 126 Wing contributed to its final annihilation on this date when it destroyed 40 more vehicles. Making up for their comparatively slow progress since D-Day, British and Canadian troops began a rapid pursuit of the enemy that would not end until they reached the Belgian city of Antwerp on 4 September.

For the next few weeks, No 126 Wing would see little aerial action, and would not score again until 18 September. Ground attack sorties continued at a rapid pace, however, and by the end of August the wing had claimed another 67 vehicles destroyed. And just as the Wehrmacht withdrew from the battlefield, so did units of the Jagdwaffe. Badly mauled, they pulled back to the Reich in order to re-equip and train new pilots in an effort to make good the horrendous losses suffered in the previous three months. D-Day and the battle for Normandy had cost the Luftwaffe 1400 aircraft and 425 pilots killed from II. *Jagdkorps* alone, with a further 250 listed as missing and 50 as PoWs.

On 1 September No 126 Wing began a series of four base moves in a week when three of its units flew to B24 St-André-de-l'Eure and No 401 Sqn headed to B28 Evreux. The following day the wing left for B26 Illiers-l'Eveque, which was already occupied by No 127 Wing. Fortunately, just as the squadrons arrived at this overcrowded base, new orders were issued and No 126 Wing found themselves at B44 Poix, near Amiens, on the 3rd. The move to B44 was one of necessity, as the short range of the Spitfire had effectively left the wing out of range of the frontline for almost a week.

On 6 September No 401 Sqn arrived at B56 Evere, near Brussels, thus becoming the first 2nd TAF unit to land on Belgian soil. The rest of No 126 Wing would follow the next day, allowing operations to quickly resume.

No 442 Sqn Spitfire IX MK304 receives a new Merlin engine at a Forward Repair Unit in France on 19 August 1944. Such outfits were a critical component of the Mobile Fighter Wing, and by the end of the Normandy campaign the Forward Repair Unit employed nearly 4000 personnel. A long-lived Spitfire, MK304 also served with Nos 310, 412 and 331 Sqns until written off in a force-landing after suffering engine failure while still assigned to the latter unit in Norway in September 1945 (*DND PL 31363*)

MARKET GARDEN AND RAIL INTERDICTION

Now firmly based in Belgium, No 126 Wing's stay at B56 Evere would ultimately last just two weeks. Operations began on 7 September, but only 30 sorties could be flown that day due to weather. Thanks to the base's close proximity to Brussels, countless dignitaries dropped by for 'a visit' with the Canadian units, as did numerous Allied fighters and bombers that got into trouble over enemy territory and could not make it back to their bases in France or England. And with 500+ Dakotas flying in and out every day with both troops and supplies, it was not uncommon to have as many as 40 aircraft in the circuit at once.

No 126 Wing's Summary of Operations for this period commented, 'Many aircraft from the UK and other aerodromes on the continent landed here from operational sorties and were interrogated, there being a total of 29 aircrew in five Mustangs, two Liberators, four Thunderbolts and four Spitfire IXBs'.

September would also be a month in which the 2nd TAF entered a new phase in the war – one it had not been fully prepared or properly trained for.

After the collapse of both the Luftwaffe and the Wehrmacht in France and the remarkable speed of the Allied pursuit of the retreating German forces, senior officers in the British and American camps were in an over optimistic state of mind. By mid-September Allied Intelligence believed that the Germans were all but finished, and that the war might very well end before 1 December. At this point 21st Army Group commander Field Marshal Bernard Montgomery proposed a plan to secure a crossing over the Rhine that would allow his armoured 'spearheads' to thrust deep into Germany and the industrial Ruhr. It was a bold plan (codenamed Operation *Market Garden*) in which three-and-a-half airborne divisions would be dropped on multiple Dutch bridges at Eindhoven, Nijmegen and Arnhem. The lightly armed paratroopers would hold these vital crossings until relieved by the tanks and infantry of the British XXX Corps.

Market Garden was to be the biggest airborne operation of the war and, remarkably, one in which the resources of the 2nd TAF would not be used. It was believed that there might be some confusion over the drop zones between the air units assigned to the airborne operations and aircraft from the 2nd TAF. Fighters based in England would provide escort for the hundreds of transports and gliders, but no ground support for the paratroopers.

Even before *Market Garden* had commenced on 17 September, there had been no battlefield preparation assigned to No 126 Wing. No bridges or road junctions were tasked for destruction. It is unsurprising, therefore, that the wing's Summary of Operations from 17 to 26 September makes no mention of *Market Garden* at all. Indeed, it was not until the very end of the battle that No 126 Wing made any real contribution, but by then it was too late for air power to save the the beleaguered paratroopers on the ground.

On the eve of the battle No 126 Wing flew 130 sorties for the destruction of three vehicles and the damaging of two locomotives. On the 17th, as the three airborne divisions began their drop and XXX Corps commenced its push north, No 126 Wing flew just 66 sorties, damaging three locomotives. The following day six aircraft of No 401 Sqn ran into 30+ Fw 190s five miles west of Venlo. 'Results of the thrash was one Fw 190 claimed destroyed by Flg Off R M Davenport (in MK266) and one damaged', recounted the Operational Summary.

'Pea soup' fog would limit the wing's activities to just 12 sorties on the 19th, although No 401 Sqn lost its CO on one of these flights. Sqn Ldr Trainor (in JK795) experienced engine failure deep inside enemy territory, and although he was able to glide his fighter some 20 miles, he was forced to bail out near Derwen and was captured. Flt Lt R I A Smith assumed command of the unit.

The following day the 'A' Party of No 126 Wing made its way to its new quarters at B68 Le Culot. This airfield was a recently liberated Luftwaffe base that had been bombed by the Allies, badly damaging its barracks. The facilities were miserable, and there was no indoor plumbing or toilets. Despite the conditions, and inconsistent weather, the wing maintained a steady pace of operations after flying in on 21 September. The following day No 401 Sqn lost two Spitfires and a pilot in a midair collision caused by poor weather. Lt Cdr A C Wallace – a Fleet Air Arm officer on attachment – was killed when his machine (ML118) hit the Spitfire of Flg Off J N G Dick (MJ563) near B66 Blankenberg. The former crashed to his death, but Dick managed to force-land at B66.

The move to B68 would at last allow No 126 Wing to undertake patrols over Arnhem and Nijmegen – they had been too far west to undertake such missions when at B56. Finally, after weeks of base moves and little real action, on 25 September, just as the last remnants of the British 1st Airborne Division were evacuated over the Rhine, 2nd TAF's fighters made their presence felt. No 126 Wing's Summary of Operations No 87 describes part of the story from that day;

'Low patrols were started by No 401 Sqn, who were airborne (12 aircraft) at 1429 hrs. This patrol covered the Arnhem–Nijmegen area to intercept enemy aircraft in that vicinity, and to protect the Nijmegen and Arnhem bridges. They encountered 30+ Fw 190s and Me 109s attempting to bomb both bridges. After a

Sqn Ldr Hugh Trainor joined the RCAF in February 1940, and after the completion of his training he was retained as an instructor until October 1942. Posted to the UK, he joined No 402 Sqn in March 1943 and became a flight commander with No 411 Sqn two months later. Following another brief spell as an instructor, Trainor rejoined No 411 Sqn in December 1943 and claimed 6.5 victories with the unit between 28 June and 4 July 1944. He became CO of No 401 Sqn the following month, claiming two more fighters destroyed on 27 and 31 July. Having seen much action since the D-Day landings, Trainor's luck finally ran out on 19 September when his aircraft suffered engine failure over enemy territory and he was forced to bail out into captivity (*DND PL 28271*)

general dogfight the score was one Fw 190 destroyed and one Me 109 damaged by Flt Lt R R Bouskill (in MJ300) and two Me 109s destroyed and one damaged by Flt Lt G W Johnson (in MH479).'

Ninety minutes later it was No 412 Sqn's turn to defend the bridges from German fighter-bombers, Flt Lt D C Laubman (in MJ393) being credited with one Fw 190 destroyed – the first of eight victories and two damaged that he would claim in just 72 hours. Flg Off H W McLeod (in NH322) also downed a Focke-Wulf fighter, but he was in turn shot up by a Bf 109 from JG 26 and forced to crash-land.

26 September would also provide No 126 Wing's No 412 Sqn with a good day's hunting. Things had not got off to a promising start, however, when heavy overnight rain left B68's runway unserviceable. Keen to 'mix it' with the Luftwaffe once again, the pilots worked alongside the groundcrews with shovels and picks as they went about filling in some of the holes that had appeared on both the taxiways and the runway. By 1100 hrs B68 was declared serviceable once again, and soon after midday No 412 Sqn commenced a high-level patrol over Venlo-Nijmegen.

German fighters – some from JG 11 – were intercepted by the unit at 1330 hrs and five Fw 190s and three Bf 109s shot down. Aces Flt Lts R I A Smith (in MJ461), D C Laubman (in MJ393) and W J Banks (in MJ223) led the way with two victories apiece, while Flg Offs P E Hurtuboise (in NH189) and P M Charron (in MK237) claimed one each. The latter pilot's Fw 190 kill gave him ace status, and he and Laubman (this time in MJ329) claimed two more Bf 109s at 1620 hrs near Nijmegen.

Operations on 27 September began early, as the Luftwaffe redoubled its efforts to destroy the bridges at Arnhem and Nijmegen. As a result No 126 Wing would record its highest tally of enemy aircraft shot down in a single day to date – the wing would also encounter Me 262s for the first time too. All four squadrons flew low patrols in the Nijmegen area, No 412 Sqn taking off first at 0728 hrs. Just northeast of Nijmegen they ran into 10+ Bf 109s and 12+ Fw 190s, and in the ensuing engagement Flt Lts Rod Smith (in MJ461) and Don Laubman (in MJ393) and Flg Off L F Berryman (in NH371) each claimed two Bf 109s destroyed apiece.

On the third patrol of the day it was No 411 Sqn's turn to add to the wing's score when its pilots ran into 15+ Fw 190s from II./JG 26 and shot down seven of them, with three more damaged. Leading the scoring was future ace Flt Lt E G Lapp (in NH174) with two kills, and singles were claimed by Flt Lts J M McConnell (in MJ852) and J M Portz (in ML300) and Flg Offs G F Mercer (in MJ240), E G Ireland (in MJ536) and L G D Pow (in NH353).

Rigger Sid Tucker inspects the battle damage inflicted to Flg Off E G Ireland's Spitfire IX MJ536 of No 411 Sqn on the morning of 27 September 1944. After shooting down his first enemy aircraft (an Fw 190) east of Nijmegen, Ireland was caught by a short burst of cannon fire from a second German fighter which badly damaged the port wing and aileron of his Spitfire. 27 September was an active day for 2nd TAF fighter units, which claimed no fewer than 45 German fighters shot down – 22 by No 126 Wing alone. MJ536 survived the war and was later sold to the Royal Netherlands Air Force in May 1947. It was written off in a crash in October of the following year (*Author's Collection via Chris Thomas*)

No 412 Sqn's second patrol shortly after noon brought further results when 40+ Fw 190s and 20+ Bf 109s attempted to get through to the bridges once again. Flg Off Berryman (again in NH371) got a Bf 109 for his third victory of the day, and fourth overall – he would finish the war with this tally. Flt Lt Laubman (in MJ393) also claimed a Bf 109, while Flt Lt C W Fox (in NH357) got two Fw 190s – his final wartime tally would be four destroyed and five damaged.

Flt Lt J M Portz of No 411 Sqn, seen here sitting on the wing of NH471/DB-J *Winnifred*, served in both North Africa and Europe. Flying a total of 244 sorties, he shot down two Fw 190s and damaged a third on 27/28 September 1944. Portz also claimed two aircraft shared destroyed, two probables and four damaged. NH471 had previously served with No 132 Sqn prior to being transferred to No 411 Sqn in August 1944, and remnants of the unit's FF codes can clearly be seen beneath the recently applied DB lettering (*Public Archives of Canada PMR 78-7*)

Squadronmate Flg Off P E Hurtuboise (in NH189) was killed, however, when his Spitfire was shot down by a German fighter near Nijmegen.

At 1330 hrs, during No 411 Sqn's second patrol of the day, Flt Lt Lapp (in NH174) and Flg Off R M Cook (in MK832) intercepted a lone Me 410 attempting to bomb the bridge at Nijmegen. They made short work of the twin-engined fighter-bomber, after which the pilots spotted four Ju 88s – the latter escaped into cloud before they could be intercepted, however.

Finally, during its third and last patrol of the day, No 412 Sqn pilots closed out the wing's tally when they chased Fw 190s from several units (including II./JG 26) all the way back to their home airfields. Flt Lt Laubman (in MJ393) claimed one destroyed to take his tally to four for the day, Flt Lt J B Doak (in NH370) also downed an Fw 190 and ace Flt Lt D R C Jamieson (in NH371) got two. The unit suffered its second fatality of 27 September during this engagement when Flg Off R Clasper (in PT405) was shot down by a fighter from JG 26 near the latter's Borkenberge airfield.

All told, No 126 Wing (specifically Nos 411 and 412 Sqns) had claimed 22 enemy fighters destroyed and ten damaged. It had been an extraordinary day, with 2nd TAF units being credited with 45 German fighters shot down overall.

Although the action was less intense on 28 September, No 411 Sqn again managed to get on the wing scoreboard when Flt Lt J M Portz (in ML300) and Flg Off M G Graham (in MJ474) shot down two of the six Fw 190s that they encountered on an early morning patrol over Nijmegen. It was No 442 Sqn's turn to engage the enemy two hours later, although its pilots could only damage a single Fw 190 and had Flt Lt G G Miller (in PL490) shot down and killed in return by I./JG 11.

Again, pilots also reported seeing 'several single- and twin-engined jet-propelled enemy aircraft, some believed to be carrying bombs, but the majority were believed to be carrying out reconnaissance missions'. Much was already known about the Me 262 by this time, and the reaction from the pilots of No 126 Wing to this potential threat showed just how well briefed they were regarding the new German jet. By October the Royal Aircraft Establishment had produced the following notes on how best to deal with the new jets;

'The outstanding advantages of the Me 262 are its high speeds, very high diving speeds and probable high ceiling, all of which give it a good performance at 35,000 ft. Its disadvantages are caused mainly by its high wing loading – namely a high take-off speed requiring a long take-off run, high stalling speed and poor manoeuvring qualities. It will also tend to overshoot its target at high speed like any jet-propelled fighter.

'The Me 262 will have the usual poor performance of a jet aircraft at low speed. Thus, it can be attacked most easily by fighters now in service when it is cruising or climbing. In manoeuvres, the Me 262 should be forced into tight turns or into a zoom climb unless the altitude at which it is encountered is near the ceiling of the attacking aircraft.'

It was also at this time that No 126 Wing exchanged its well-worn Spitfire IXBs for No 125 Wing's newer Mk IXEs. The only difference between the two models was the wing armament, as the Mk IXE boasted two 20 mm cannon and two 0.50-in Browning machine guns, thus giving it a heavier punch.

There was more fighting over Nijmegen on 29 September, despite worsening weather conditions as the day progressed. A low-level patrol by 13 aircraft from No 401 Sqn ran into a 'gaggle' of 30+ Fw 190s and Bf 109s at 1030 hrs and claimed nine Messerschmitt fighters shot down. Flt Lts R I A Smith (in MJ448) and H J Everard (in MJ565) and Flg Offs J C Hughes (in MK577) and D F Husband (in ML260 each claimed two kills, and Flt Lt R R Bouskill (in MJ300) one. The victories for Everard and Husband gave them ace status, both pilots having joined No 401 Sqn with kills from previous units. The squadron suffered one fatality in return when Flg Off C G Hutchings (in NH404) was shot down and killed by an enemy fighter.

Next into the fray at 1145 hrs were ten aircraft from No 412 Sqn that were performing the second of the unit's three patrols that day. Some 50+ Fw 190s were encountered east of Nijmegen at 8000-9000 ft, three of which were claimed destroyed by Flg Offs W A Aziz

Sqn Ldr Rod Smith's MJ448/YO-W sits with other No 401 Sqn aircraft in the muddy dispersal area at B84 Rips in October 1944. The Malta ace would shoot down six Bf 109s between 27 and 29 September, with the last two being claimed in this aircraft. Smith was flying MK577/YO-F when he helped bring down the RAF's first Me 262 on 5 October, however. Another Spitfire that survived the war, MJ448 was sold to Turkey in May 1947 (*Author's Collection via Chris Thomas*)

(in PL204) and D R C Jamieson (in NH371) and Plt Off W C Busby (in PL438) – the latter pilot subsequently ran out of fuel and crash-landed near Hacht.

After five hectic days the weather closed in during the afternoon of 29 September and No 126 Wing saw no action the following day. Nevertheless, it had been an impressive showing by the four units at B68. They had registered 52 victories for the month, which was half of the overall total for No 83 Group during this period. The RCAF's other Spitfire outfit, No 125 Wing, came in second within 2nd TAF with 38 victories. The top unit overall was No 412 Sqn, which destroyed 29 enemy aircraft – eight of them were credited to Flt Lt Don Laubman in just three days, four on 27 September. His closest rival was Flt Lt Rod Smith with six enemy fighters destroyed during the same period.

Yet despite these successes in the air, on the ground Operation *Market Garden* had ended in ignominious defeat for the Allies. Indeed, it was one of the worst reversals inflicted on British and American forces in World War 2, with 17,200 casualties. To put this figure into perspective, the Allies had suffered 10,000 casualties during the D-Day landings. Even with air superiority over the battlefield, the airborne forces were unable to reach, and hold, their objectives.

There were many reasons for the failure of this operation, but perhaps the most crucial one was the speed at which the Wehrmacht was able to assemble and then commit units into battle. They were aided in their endeavours by the Allied insistence that all offensive air assets had to protect the airborne landing zones exclusively, thus leaving the Germans free to move reinforcements into surrounding areas almost completely unhampered by air attack.

ON THE MOVE AGAIN

The beginning of October saw No 126 Wing changing airfields once again in what was its seventh move since D-Day. The advance party reached B84 Rips, in Holland, on 1 October, with two units flying in on the 3rd and the others following suit the next day.

In the air, the month got off to a bad start when Plt Off D E Reiber (in ML351) was killed in a crash near Hess on the 1st whilst undertaking a weather flight. The following day No 401 Sqn lost a pilot and two aircraft when they were bounced by four Fw 190s from II./JG 26. The unit had spotted a similar number of Focke-Wulfs over Nijmegen Bridge, and when the Canadian pilots gave chase they were hit from above. Five-victory ace Flt Lt Russ Bouskill (in MJ300) was killed and WO M Thomas (in MJ726) bailed out over B80. On a more positive note, and providing a portent of things to come, No 442 Sqn's Flg Off F B Young (in PL423) claimed an Me 262 damaged over Nijmegen.

A flightline of Spitfires from No 411 Sqn at B84 Rips in October 1944. No 126 Wing's stay at this airfield was a short one – 4 to 13 October. Described as a 'mudhole', all personnel were happy when the order to move arrived (*Author's Collection via Brian Jeffery Street*)

Flt Lt (later Sqn Ldr) R I A Smith joined No 412 Sqn in March 1944 after spending two months as a supernumerary at No 401 Sqn. Having claimed six kills flying Spitfires with No 126 Sqn during the defence of Malta in 1942, he added a further five as a flight commander with No 412 Sqn from 7 July to 27 September 1944. Given command of No 401 Sqn, Smith claimed two and one shared kills with this unit, including a quarter-share in the first Me 262 shot down by Allied fighter pilots. He ended the war with 13 and 1 shared destroyed, 1 shared probable and 1 damaged to his name (*DND PL 29398*)

5 October began with high patrols of the Arnhem-Nijmegen area by aircraft of No 412 Sqn. Later in the day aircraft from No 401 Sqn would make history. Twelve fighters from the unit had begun their patrol at 1353 hrs, and what happened next is briefly described in No 126 Wing's Summary of Operations for that day;

'The aircraft, led by Sqn Ldr R I A Smith (in MK577) sighted an Me 262 at 1445 hrs diving towards Nijmegen. The squadron went in to attack and the enemy aircraft was destroyed, shared between Smith, Flt Lt R M Davenport (in ML269), Flt Lt H J Everard (in MJ852), Flg Off J MacKay (in MJ726) and Flg Off A L Sinclair (in MK698). The enemy aircraft seemed inclined to show fight and returned fire on many occasions but hit nothing. The enemy aircraft burned in the air and crashed in friendly territory at E655588. It is believed that this is the first jet-propelled aircraft to be destroyed by RAF or RCAF fighters. The squadron landed at 1508 hrs.'

It was a moment of triumph, the pilots involved 'chattering like magpies' as they compared notes and relived the experience of downing an Me 262 from I./KG 51. No 83 Group HQ issued a bulletin confirming its pilots were the first to shoot down a German jet, but was that statement true? The first Me 262 victory was credited jointly to Maj Joseph Myers and 2Lt Manford Croy of the P-47D-equipped 78th Fighter Group (FG), who manoeuvred a 1./KG 51 machine into the ground west of Brussels on 28 August 1944 without actually firing a single round at it. A similar thing happened on 2 October 1944 when P-47D pilot 1Lt Valmore Beaudrault of the 365th FG ran an Me 262 out of fuel in low-level pursuit near Dusseldorf. Astoundingly, the pilot of the jet on both occasions was Oberfeldwebel Hieronymous Lauer, who survived both encounters! No 401 Sqn's success on 5 October was, therefore, the first to involve an exchange of fire between the combatants.

6 October dawned crisp and clear, and patrols were off early starting at 0617 hrs. Most of those flown by No 126 Wing were uneventful, with only a locomotive damaged and a few vehicles left as 'smokers' during the morning. It was not until 1500 hrs when No 442 Sqn was undertaking its final mission of the day that things finally heated up;

All that was left of No 401 Sqn's Me 262, shot down five miles northeast of Nijmegen on 5 October 1944. The aircraft, Werk-Nr 170093, was being flown by Hauptmann Hans Christoff Buttmann of 3./KG 51 at the time. Although he managed to bail out, Buttmann was too low and his parachute did not have time to deploy. An Intelligence officer can be seen examining the wreckage in the foreground while the Royal Engineers pump water out of the crater (*Author's Collection*)

'442's last patrol proved to be fruitful and very eventful from the first mix-up with enemy aircraft until in the circuit. They had a thrash with some 100+ Fw 190s and Me 109s from 25,000 ft up to 28,000 ft five miles northeast of Nijmegen. This proved fruitful to the score of three destroyed and four damaged and all our pilots returning. Flg Offs S M McClarty (in NH588) and E T Hoare (in PL207) downed an Me 109 each and Flg Off D W Goodwin (in NH556) got an Fw 190.

'The eventful part of the mission actually came when they were bounced three times by Spitfires. Firstly at Nijmegen when two Spits bounced them, secondly south of Nijmegen when one Spit bounced Yellow section and the third time when an unidentified Spit attacked and damaged Flt Lt McClarty's aircraft in the circuit over base. We ended up with three Spits Cat "B".'

No 412 Sqn would also sight 'unidentified Spits with no markings but a darker camouflage to ours' on the last patrol of the day.

High patrols over the Arnhem-Nijmegen area continued on the 7th, and early in the day No 442 Sqn reported 'four Me 262s sighted at 20,000 ft but our aircraft could not close'. Several hours later two more jets were spotted over the field at 15,000 ft. No 442 Sqn finally got to grips with the enemy on the last of its four patrols at 1635 hrs, when 35+ Fw 190s from I. and II./JG 26 were intercepted by 11 Spitfires 'going west at 18,000-20,000 ft' east of Cleve. In the ensuing dogfight Flg Off F B Young (in PL260) destroyed two – the last of his four kills with the unit – and Flg Off J P Lumsden (in PL330) claimed one.

For the next six days 'duff weather' would ground the wing. While the Allies enjoyed both strategic and tactical air superiority, European weather proved to be the Germans' best asset. It gave them time to repair rail links, move men and supplies both day and night and bolster their frontline defences. While the tactical air forces were able to inflict damage on the German transportation system, thus hindering the movement of men and supplies, it was the weather that in many cases restored the balance in the enemy's favour. The rain also covered the airstrip in several inches of water, making operations impossible. Indeed, aircraft just standing in their dispersal areas were sinking!

No 411 Sqn departed B84 on 13 October for a ten-day Air Firing Course at RAF Warmwell, in Dorset. It was a chance for battle-weary pilots to hone their strafing and dive-bombing skills in a quiet environment and, more importantly, to rest up after many months of near constant combat. The following day the rest of No 126 Wing was on the move once again. 'A' Party 'pushed off at 0930 hrs from B84 at Rips to its new site at B80 Volkel. Int/Ops and Flying Control were able to function in a fashion by 1230 hrs'. No sorties were flown, however, due to persistent bad weather.

The first victories scored by No 402 Sqn with the Spitfire XIV came on 6 October 1945 while the unit was still assigned to No 125 Wing. Flt Lt A R Speare, pictured here, was credited with his one and only aerial victory of the war on that day when he shot down an Fw 190 southwest of Nijmegen while flying RM682. The squadron's total for the 6th was five enemy fighters destroyed. The first victory scored by No 402 Sqn after it had joined No 126 Wing was claimed on 8 February 1945 by Flt Lt K S Sleep (in RM862), who downed a Ju 88 near Coesfeld (*DND PL 33032*)

No 411 Sqn pilots at the ready at B80 Volkel in late October 1944. They are, from left to right, Flt Lt J J Boyle, Flg Offs C D W Wilson and A C McNiece and Flt Lt R A Gilberstad. Boyle finished the war as an ace with five and one shared kills (including an Me 262) and one damaged in the air, and two destroyed and one damaged on the ground. Wilson would claim two destroyed and one damaged with No 411 Sqn, followed by three destroyed and one damaged in 1948 while flying Spitfires with the Israeli Defence Force. Gilberstad claimed one destroyed and one damaged (*Public Archives of Canada PL 42923*)

Airmen pose for a photograph after hanging 1000 lbs of bombs on this No 442 Sqn Spitfire in late 1944. The weapons lack contact fuses, which suggests that they are each fitted with a delay fuse in the tail assembly. The 250-lb bomb (seen here under the fighter's wings) was of questionable tactical value due to its low explosive weight (*Public Archives of Canada PMR 76-372*)

After nearly a week of no operational flying, the wing commenced its rail interdiction programme on 15 October. All three squadrons packed in two missions each pre-lunch before the weather deteriorated once again. For these operations the Spitfires carried a single 500-lb bomb (fitted with a 0.25-second delay fuse) beneath the fuselage. No 401 Sqn dropped 23 bombs that morning, followed by No 442 Sqn with 19 and No 412 Sqn with 16. No 442 Sqn had the best showing of the day in terms of results, destroying 15 railway cars and damaging a locomotive. The Operational Summary also noted that 'the pilots were rusty – or completely inexperienced' when it came to dive-bombing.

Weather once again played its hand and grounded the wing for a day on the 16th, and only 14 sorties were generated the following day. This downtime gave the pilots the chance to see their latest combat films, including those of the Me 262 shot down by No 401 Sqn on 5 October.

The weather cleared at last on 18 October, being deemed to be 'comparatively good for this neck of the woods' according to the Operational Summary. All three squadrons put in three 'shows' with encouraging results. Rail interdiction was the order of the day, but due to a shortage of 500-lb bombs the last two missions saw Spitfires equipped with lighter and less effective 250-lb bombs. Nevertheless, the main railway line between Münster and Haltern was cut in three places, while the junction near Dulmen received eight direct hits and three near misses. By dusk No 126 Wing had dropped 69 500-lb and 73 250-lb bombs, resulting in 12 locomotives being listed as 'Cat B', 11 as 'Cat C' and eight mechanised transports noted as destroyed.

The next day the battle with the weather continued, and it was not until 1358 hrs that the first flights got airborne. It was also the first time that No 126 Wing had loaded its Spitfires with 1000 lbs of bombs – one 500-lb weapon under the fuselage and two 250 'pounders' under the wings. The Operational Summary noted, 'The honour of dropping

such a load for the first time went to Flt Lt "Tex" Davenport and Flg Off Cliff Wyman, both of No 401 Sqn. They located a train with 25 goods trucks loaded with large boxes near Coesfeld and bombed from 8000 ft down to 3000 ft. The score was "near misses", resulting in a request to take the whole squadron next time, which was done'. 19 October was also the second day in a row that all squadrons reported intense flak at various points in their missions.

Bad weather continued to hamper the wing's dive-bombing efforts on the 20th, although 77 operational sorties were flown nevertheless. However, few targets could be found, and those that were were obscured by enough cloud to make good results impossible. A total of 120 500-lb bombs were dropped for one locomotive damaged and nine transports destroyed. The rail interdiction offensive continued unabated.

The weather that was affecting No 126 Wing was also keeping the Luftwaffe from showing itself. To date the wing had shot down just four enemy aircraft in October, and having now been given the task of dropping bombs on enemy targets, the chance of spotting Luftwaffe aircraft was even more limited. A quote from the Summary of Operations for 24 October sheds some light on the wing's bombing activities during this period, and what the pilots and groundcrews felt about this revised mission;

'The boys were a little reluctant at first to see their trim, neat, streamlined Spitfire being loaded down with bomb racks under the fuselage. Then came the wing racks, which did not improve on the kite's beauty, and meant another 500-lb load on this great little fighter. The pride came back though in seeing this little aircraft go out there and take it. As the boys' bombing has improved and their results have begun to pile up, not in enemy aircraft but in locomotives, railways, bridges and crossings, so has their keenness in going out after these targets improved, till now we take second place to none in these shows and the Army says "Thanks a Million".'

This day would also see the awarding of more 'well-earned gongs'. For their participation and action in the Battle of Falaise and the

With an airman giving his pilot directions, VZ-H of No 412 Sqn is taxied out fully loaded with 1000 lbs of bombs at B80 Volkel. This photograph would have been taken on or after 19 October 1944 – the first time Spitfires of No 126 Wing carried a 500-lb and two 250-lb bombs as a full load. It was a heavy burden for the Spitfire to bear, and the structural stresses endured by the fighter when bombed up resulted in many 'wrinkled' wings. The latter could be quickly replaced, however, as there was a plentiful supply held at Forward Repair Units (*Author's Collection*)

When No 442 Sqn joined No 126 Wing on 15 July 1944, its CO was Sqn Ldr Harry Dowding. He would remain in command until September 1944, when he ended his second tour. Dowding did not score any kills while flying with No 126 Wing, although did end the war with five and three shared victories and three damaged to his name. All bar two of his kills and one damaged were claimed with No 403 Sqn in 1943 (*DND PI 28938*)

No 411 Sqn pilots pose with their CO, Sqn Ldr Bob Hayward (back row left), shortly before he handed over command of the unit to Sqn Ldr E G Lapp (*Public Archives of Canada PMR 78-311*)

'Arnhem Air Battle', Sqn Ldrs Charlie Trainor and Bob Hayward would receive Distinguished Service Orders. Sqn Ldrs Harry Dowding and Dean Dover and Flt Lt Bill Klersy were awarded Bars to their DFCs and Flt Lt 'Tex' Davenport, Flt Lt Russ Bouskill and Flg Off Lloyd Berryman received DFCs.

On 28 October the weather forecasters predicted good flying conditions. Only two units – Nos 412 and 442 Sqns – would participate in the day's actions, and much credit must be given to the groundcrews for their all-out effort in turning aircraft around between missions. Thanks to their hard work, in ten hours of operations 81 sorties were flown, and the results achieved were impressive. On the seventh bombing mission of the day at 1420 hrs, No 412 Sqn spotted Fw 190s from II./JG 26 returning to base after engaging Typhoon IBs from No 182 Sqn. Flt Lt Don Laubman (in PL186) succeeded in downing two of the German fighters, thus taking his final victory tally to 14 and two shared kills and three damaged. Laubman was now the top-scoring Canadian pilot still on operations, and also 2nd TAF's leading scorer since D-Day.

At 1515 hrs No 412 Sqn, on its eighth mission of the day, intercepted Bf 109Gs from III./JG 26 just as they took off from Hohenbudberg. Flt Lt P M Charron (in MH882) claimed two destroyed to take his final tally to seven.

Aside from scoring four aerial victories, Nos 412 and 442 Sqns had also dropped 159 500-lb bombs that caused 20 rail cuts, knocked out one locomotive and damaged 22 others and destroyed seven vehicles. But these results came at a price, for pilots attacking ground targets faced a double threat.

Firstly, German flak was always deadly, remaining remarkably efficient right up until the end of the war. On the 28th a battery near Haltern brought down No 442 Sqn's Flg Off G A Costello (in PL207), who perished despite bailing out of his fighter. Secondly, pilots always ran the risk of being mistakenly hit by Allied ground fire. Such a fate befell Flg Off Costello's squadronmate Flt Lt W B Randall (in MJ466), who bailed out near Dorsten and was captured.

During a strafing attack any bullets that hit a hard surface would ricochet in all directions – in some cases right back at the source. And because the Spitfire had its glycol cooling radiators located on the underside of the wings, they were extremely vulnerable. If the radiator was hit it was only a matter of time before the engine would seize and burst into flames.

Two more fighters were lost on 29 October, again to flak, while implementing the rail interdiction programme. One of those was flown by No 442 Sqn CO, Sqn Ldr

W A Olmsted (MJ397), whose 500-lb bomb failed to come off when he attacked a bridge over the Dortmund Canal. The weapon finally dropped away when he was strafing a lorry, the blast from the bomb destroying the vehicle and badly damaging his Spitfire. Olmsted immediately realised that he had no elevator or aileron control, leaving the rudder as the only flying surface that would work properly. He managed to coax the ailing fighter back 100 miles to friendly territory, whereupon its Merlin seized and he bailed out. The line at the bottom of the Operational Summary for the day was brief and succinct;

'Losses – Sqn Ldr Olmsted 442 hit by own bomb blast and bailed out successfully. Returned to base an hour or two later.'

Olmsted himself noted in his logbook that by the end of October he had gone through seven Spitfires because of repeated flak damage.

29 October also saw No 411 Sqn lose Flg Off T F Kinsler (in PV240), who was killed when his fighter was hit by flak during a strafing attack on a train near Metelen. The Spitfire was seen to crash in flames.

As the weather in Holland worsened, the wing adjusted its tactics to better suit the conditions. Instead of sending out a complete squadron of 12 aircraft, squadrons switched to despatching four- and six-aircraft flights. These proved more manageable in the circumstances, and were still deemed to be robust enough to defend themselves should enemy fighters be encountered.

While vital in helping Allied armies advance towards Germany, the ground attack sorties flown by the Spitfire units in the autumn of 1944 were hard on both pilots and groundcrews, as Sqn Ldr Olmsted explained;

'It was at Volkel that the true temperament and grim determination of the pilots was revealed. Flying an aircraft that was never built for dive-bombing, and therefore could withstand very little punishment from flak, attacking the most heavily defended targets in the world, operating under the worst possible weather conditions, but displaying an inexpressible keenness and desire to do a successful job, they never failed to earn frequent commendations from AVM Harry Broadhurst, ACM Sir Arthur Tedder and other Allied commanders.'

No 411 Sqn's full complement of pilots come together for the camera soon after the unit moved to B80 Volkel in October 1944. Future ace Flt Lt R J Audet is standing directly in front of the VHF aerial. Autumn ushered in some of the worst weather of the war, severely disrupting flying. Indeed, No 126 Wing claimed just six aerial victories for the entire month (*Public Archives of Canada PMR 78-248*)

November saw little improvement in the weather, and this meant that pilots were in a constant state of readiness waiting for a break in the conditions. On the first day of the month only 18 sorties were flown, but on the 2nd No 442 Sqn added to the wing's tally of aerial victories with two Fw 190s shot down. The Canadian pilots had just bombed their target southeast of Coesfeld when they spotted the German fighters and attacked. Plt Off J P W Francis (in PL324) claimed one of the Focke-Wulfs and Flt Lt M E Jowsey (in MJ463) downed the other. The latter's success gave him ace status, as he had joined No 442 Sqn in late September with four victories to his name following a tour with No 92 Sqn in North Africa the previous year.

In a repeat of the incident that befell Sqn Ldr Olmsted four days earlier, No 442 Sqn's Flt Lt R B Barker (in PL436) had a bomb hang up that later fell away and exploded while he was strafing a train. The Spitfire was badly damaged, although the pilot managed to limp back to B80 and land, after which the fighter was listed Category 'E' (a write off).

On the morning of 4 November the fair weather allowed No 411 Sqn to get off early. The unit's target was a road/rail crossover and bridge just west of Wesel. The section led by Flt Lt Crawford put all of its bombs in the target area, with one direct hit on the railway line itself. This pattern continued throughout the day, with No 442 Sqn joining the party. The third mission was led by Sqn Ldr Olmsted, his section cutting the flyover at Dulmen, with direct hits also being registered on dual railway lines in the area – a locomotive and a truck were destroyed by the violent explosion.

Unfortunately, Flg Off F B Young's Spitfire (RR194) was also hit by the debris from the direct hits and he was seen to bail out. He landed safely, but too close to a German flak battery that had just been strafed. The gunners vented their anger on Young by severely beating him – he spent the rest of the war as a PoW.

It had been a busy day for No 126 Wing, with 88 sorties flown by Nos 411 and 442 Sqns and 167 500-lb bombs dropped.

SPITFIRE AS A DIVE-BOMBER

The development and formation of the Allied Tactical Air Forces was a shining example of ingenuity and cooperation. A huge amount of thought and energy was spent on the organisational aspects of these forces – command and control, logistics and supply, airfield construction etc.

In June 1944 the Western Allies had 9000+ aircraft in their various tactical air forces, with 2000+ in the 2nd TAF alone. The majority of these were single-seat fighters such as the Spitfire and Typhoon. Both types were 'adapted' for the fighter-bomber role, and of the two the Spitfire was the least capable. Its light weight and short range limited its bomb load – the Typhoon could haul 2000 lbs of bombs, but the Spitfire only half that amount. This meant that on most of missions flown by Spitfires in No 126 Wing, just a single 500-lb bomb was carried. It was found that the effect of two additional 250-lb bombs under the wings was negligible, and they hindered accuracy. And when the Spitfire did carry bombs its range was considerably shorter.

No 401 Sqn Spitfires taxi towards the runway at B80, each fighter being accompanied by an 'erk' whose job it was to prevent the unsighted pilot in the cockpit from running into the Spitfire in front of him. A single 500-lb bomb has been affixed to the centreline bomb rack of each fighter (*Author's Collection via Chris Thomas*)

The Spitfire IXB's armament of two 20 mm cannon and four 0.303-in machine guns was also the lightest of all the Allied fighter-bombers, although this was rectified in the later Mk IXE when two 0.50-in machine guns were fitted in place of the 0.303-in weapons.

Dive-bombing attacks early in the war had demonstrated just how effective this method was. And while the RAF and the Air Ministry were hostile to the idea of dive-bombers, the dive-bombing method was quickly adopted as the best and only way for a fighter-bomber to get bombs on target. Despite its official opposition, the RAF had in fact successfully equipped several squadrons with Vultee Vengeance dive-bombers in Burma and India. It had also seen how effective the USAAF's A-36 dive-bomber (a modified version of the P-51A) was in Sicily and Italy in 1943.

Like most Allied fighters, the Spitfire was equipped to carry bombs. Unfortunately, the bomb racks fitted to the aircraft were designed for level bombing and the bombs themselves built to be dropped from a lumbering Lancaster or Halifax flying horizontally at medium to high altitude, rather than released from a fighter diving near vertically at high-speed towards the ground. The Spitfire also lacked a proper dive-bombing sight, which meant that the pilot had to line himself up with his aim point through his gunsight – the latter was optimised for firing at aerial targets.

One of the Spitfire's greatest assets was its speed, but when in a dive this was also a problem. All the fighters hastily 'modified' into dive-bombers lacked dive brakes. The latter allowed a dive-bomber to maintain a set speed when in a dive, thus greatly increasing bombing accuracy. However, when a Spitfire was in a dive it gained speed rapidly to the point where it often exceeded 450 mph. This usually dictated higher release altitudes – above 4000 ft – so that the pilot had sufficient time and height to pull out. The Spitfire was not stressed for this vital high-g manoeuvre after dropping its bomb.

Despite these serious drawbacks, fighter-bombers carried out many effective dive-bombing attacks, although the missions required more aircraft, more sorties and many more bombs to satisfactorily complete them than would have been the case had purpose-built dive-bombers been used instead.

Operational Research (OR) studies prior to D-Day showed that bombs dropped from fighter-bombers were found to hit a viaduct 500 yards long and eight yards wide just once in 82 attempts! And near misses, it was found, did little damage. Where the fighter-bomber did excel was strafing. OR research reported it to be 'outstandingly successful' for damaging or destroying soft-skin vehicles. The only dedicated dive-bomber used over western Europe was the American SBD Dauntless, this US Navy inspired aircraft being employed in modest numbers by the French Air Force in support of the Free French Army. Between December 1944 and May 1945 a small number of SBDs flew a total of 1500 sorties and dropped 500 tons of bombs for the loss of just five aircraft.

Simply put, the Spitfire was never built for dive-bombing. The results it did achieve were more a testament to the skill of the pilots who flew it, rather than the aircraft itself.

FIGHTER BOMBER TACTICS

The following descriptions (and diagrams) describe the methods used by 2nd TAF Spitfire units, and they are taken from the report titled *Tactical Paper No 4 – Tactics used by Spitfire Day Fighter/Bomber Squadron of the 2nd TAF during the Campaign in Western Europe*;

DIVE BOMBING

Approach – the approach to the attack was made in level flight at 220-230 mph. At the moment when the target hid itself under the wing on a line of about one-third from the end of the wingtip, the pilot made a gentle turn under the horizon in the direction of the target (see diagram to right). He regulated the speed of the turn so that the target was visible all the time. This turn had to be a very steady one, and made without the excessive use of the rudder, so that the pilot could very quickly catch the target in his sight. There was another method of flying straight at the target and attacking it from a half-roll, but in this case the aircraft gathered high speed and the pilot had great difficulty steadying it and bringing it on the target.

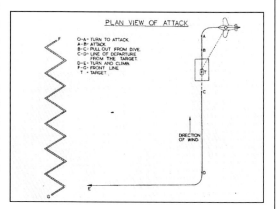

Attack – the attack was usually carried out from a dive and at an angle of 60 to 45 degrees. The leader dove at a steep angle, while the aircraft who were behind him and at his side were forced to dive at a shallower angle. When diving the pilots had to remember the danger of a traverse, as in this case the bombing was inaccurate. He also had to make sure that the aircraft did not accelerate into high speed, as the aiming time would pass too quickly and the pulling out from the dive would be much more difficult and unpleasant. The bombs were released at 3000 ft. The angle of release for the bombs depended on the direction and strength of the wind (see diagram to right)

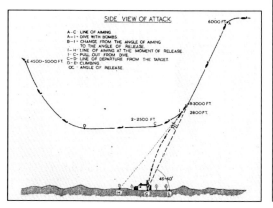

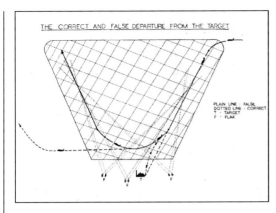

THE CORRECT AND FALSE DEPARTURE FROM THE TARGET

PLAIN LINE - FALSE
DOTTED LINE - CORRECT
T - TARGET
F - FLAK

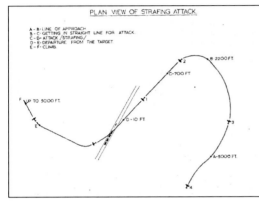

PLAN VIEW OF STRAFING ATTACK.

A - B - LINE OF APPROACH.
B - C - GETTING IN STRAIGHT LINE FOR ATTACK.
C - D - ATTACK /STRAFING/
D - E - DEPARTURE FROM THE TARGET.
E - F - CLIMB.

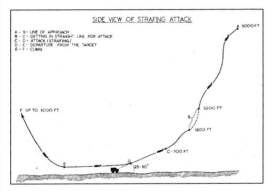

SIDE VIEW OF STRAFING ATTACK.

A - B - LINE OF APPROACH.
B - C - GETTING IN STRAIGHT LINE FOR ATTACK.
C - D - ATTACK /STRAFING/
D - E - DEPARTURE FROM THE TARGET.
E - F - CLIMB.

Departure – the departure from the target after bombing was carried out in level flight at full boost in order to get out as quickly as possible from the orbit of enemy flak. Only after having travelled some distance did the pilot start to climb. Climbing immediately after the release of bombs was one of the most common mistakes and resulted in unnecessary danger to the pilot from enemy flak. It also caused the pilot to "Black Out" and inflicted wing wrinkling on the aircraft (see diagram to left).

Strafing – the attack followed these general lines. After locating the target, the leader of the formation decided on the time, place and way of approach, passing the information by R/T to the rest of the pilots. The enemy had lookouts on all his transport vehicles. On motor transport he normally had two – one on the mudguard and one on the roof or at the back of the vehicle in question. As soon as our aircraft were sighted the vehicle usually hid under trees or in the vicinity of buildings. Thus the pilots were forced to leave the moving vehicles and not attack until they were on a part of the road where they could not easily find cover. The attack had to be carried out rapidly so as to deny the vehicle time to find cover.

The approach to attack was usually carried out from a wide turn with a loss of height so that when levelling out for the attack, the aircraft should not be higher than 1500 ft, and as far as possible at normal speed. After steadying the aircraft and getting the target squarely in the sights, the pilot would open fire at a height of about 700 ft from a distance of about 500 yards and at an angle of 25 to 30 degrees. The angle of attack in relation to the direction of the moving target used to vary from 0 to 90 degrees, being dependent mainly on the nature of the target, its position and the outlines of the terrain (see diagrams to left). The attacks on motor transport and locomotives were normally carried out as far as possible at an angle of 30 degrees from the front.

The departure from the target after the attack was carried out at full throttle, low-level flying for about 30 seconds with a turn in order to get out of the line of fire from the next aircraft. Thus, in the case of a convoy, the leader would attack the first car on the side to which he intended to turn after carrying out his attack.

Effectiveness of the cannon and machine guns in the Spitfire IX was very great, especially in attacks on road and rail transport or moving columns of enemy troops. Attacks on trains usually exploded the locomotive. The shooting up and destruction of the rail trucks, however, depended on the freight they were carrying. The attacks on road transport usually set fire to vehicles and completely destroyed them.

How accurate were the strafing attacks? To find out the OR Section produced a report titled *2nd TAF/ ORS Report No 14 – The Accuracy of Ground Strafing/ Assessment of Combat Films – December 1944 to March 1945*. It concluded;

'In general, ground strafing results are good. At least 40 percent of locomotive attacks and 30 percent of motor transport attacks are well executed, accurate and effective. A further 50 percent of the attacks, although less accurate, result in hits on the target, with consequent damage. The most noticeable errors in shooting and tactics are sweeping across or pulling through the target (17 percent of all attacks reveal this type of error), opening fire too soon, with the consequent waste of ammunition (some attacks commence at between 1000 and 2000 yards' range and last for as long as five or ten seconds) and firing for far too short a period.'

While the strafing results generally looked good on gun camera film, the fact remained that locomotives were difficult to destroy as they proved to be readily repairable. A report produced by No 83 Group, dated 16 March 1945, revealed as much;

'The information given in these notes is based on an examination of detailed records kept by the French railway authorities of about 300 attacks on locomotives with cannon and machine guns. The investigations show that strafing attacks can do serious damage to a locomotive when properly carried out. While, therefore, it is not intended to dictate tactics, it is felt that pilots would like to know the lessons learned, and where locomotives are most vulnerable.

'Of the 300 cases examined, most of which were attacked by more than one aircraft, no locomotives were destroyed. Eighty percent were damaged to a greater or lesser degree, and twenty percent were not hit at all. There was a noticeable lack of success in attacks "made on the deck".

'The average time taken to repair the strafing damage was three weeks in the period before the general attacks on repair depots by Bomber Command. After this period the average time of repair was more than six weeks.

'In November 1944, there were still 35 un-repaired locomotives which had been damaged in May/June 1944. This was due not so much to the severity of the strafing damage, but to the fact that the destruction of the locomotive depots by Bomber Command made it impossible to deal with all the repairs.

'Strafing also reduced the number of trains being run by day, thus hampering the enemy effort. Heavy casualties were also inflicted on locomotive crews, resulting in demands for armour plate protection for cabins. After a successful fighter attack, the damaged locomotive had to be taken to a repair depot, where it could be finished off by Bomber Command.

'A locomotive is a fairly thick-skinned target, but it has several vulnerable areas. Of these, the most important, and also the largest, are the firebox and boiler. Hits in other parts can normally be repaired quickly, and may not even immobilise the locomotive. The main point of aim should therefore be midway between the funnel and the front of the cabin.

'It will be seen therefore that although it is probably too much to expect to destroy locomotives with cannon and machine guns, heavy damage and dislocation can be caused.'

When one adds to the equation the fact that the Germans had 63,000 locomotives in all of Europe, and for every wagon destroyed ten replaced them – the Germans owned two million in Europe – the task of destroying rail traffic proved daunting for the young pilots of No 126 Wing. While the results of the anti-rail campaign may not, therefore, have been decisive, they did constrict German supply movements and add to the general misery suffered by German ground troops.

'The weather caused much uncertainty as usual but operations got underway shortly after a weather recce reported fair conditions in certain area', recalled the Operational Summary on 7 November. As was often the case, the day began like so many others with the weather calling the shots. Bad visibility hampered many of the attacks and the results were poor. Eighty sorties were flown, with 146 500-lb bombs being dropped for a return of just five rail cuts and two locomotives damaged.

No 442 Sqn had another pilot killed during a dive-bombing operation near Rheine, Flg Off W S Curtis (in NH556) being seen to crash into woods immediately east of Burgsteinfurt. It was thought that his aeroplane had been struck by light flak from that area, and no parachute was spotted.

Over the next three days No 126 Wing managed to fly 96 sorties for limited results. Things improved on 11 November;

'The wing put in its most sorties since the long summer days, with each unit doing the equivalent of three full squadron shows. However, of the 109 sorties flown, only a few scored any direct hits on rail lines, and enemy transport, either rail or road, offered very scarce pickings indeed.'

Heavy rain and 'duff' weather curtailed operations for the next two days. Remarkably, the weather improved on the 19th, the day dawning sunny and clear. This was described as 'good for morale all round', but the upbeat mood at B80 would be short lived. Each squadron turned in nine missions, 'knocking the wing's serviceability "into a cock-eyed hat" in short order'. Their efforts centred again on enemy road and rail transport. Attacks against road transports were impressive, but rail cuts were much harder to achieve. Lack of practice, high winds and intense flak all contributed to poor results on the day.

Up to this point in the conflict the wing had enjoyed an outstanding run of good fortune. However, the law of averages would catch up with No 412 Sqn (recently returned from APC in England) that day. The unit would perform nine operations on the 19th, and during an early mission Flg Off W H L Bellingham (in PL159) was killed while dive-bombing rail targets near Geldern. At 1335 hrs seven-kill ace Flt Lt Phil Charron (in PL245) led his second mission of the day. His flight's target was a railway bridge near Veen, and after making their bombing runs Flg Off W Cowan (in NH357) spotted 40+ Fw 190s from 5./JG 26 just as the Spitfire pilots were attempting to form up.

Without hesitation Charron called out 'lets get into the bastards', but the German fighters had both the element of surprise and the

Flt Lt Phil Charron of No 412 Sqn had claimed two Ju 88s destroyed and a Bf 109 damaged in October 1942 while flying with No 126 Sqn in the defence of Malta. Upon his return to the UK in early 1943, he spent much of the year instructing, prior to being posted to No 412 Sqn in November. Charron almost immediately returned to Canada on leave, but returned in April 1944 and then saw considerable action following D-Day. Made a flight commander in late September shortly after becoming an ace, Charron led his section of four Spitfires against 40+ German fighters on 19 November and was duly shot down and killed (*DND PL 28285*)

strength in numbers. Cowan's Spitfire was struck right away, forcing him to flee back to Volkel. Within two minutes Charron, Flg Off J W Johnston (in PL130) and and WO J A Comeau (in PL204) had all been shot down. Only Comeau survived to become a PoW.

21 November saw another full day of rail interdiction sorties, during which the wing adopted a new tactic. Squadrons would now operate in formations of eight aircraft instead of the usual four. While one formation bombed the target the other would provide top cover. This gave additional security against the roving gaggles of German fighters that were now appearing with more frequency over the battlefield.

Spitfires of Nos 401 and 411 Sqns took off at 0910 hrs and headed for a rail junction at Xanten. A dozen Fw 190s were soon spotted, followed by 12 more. As soon as the pilots had jettisoned their bombs, they turned into the Fw 190s, two of which were shot down. No 401 Sqn's Flt Lts W C Connell (in MK791) and E B Sheehy (in ML370) shared in the destruction of one fighter and No 411 Sqn's Flt Lt H A Crawford (in PK992) claimed the other. The first Fw 190 shot down represented No 126 Wing's 200th aerial victory. A trophy had been prepared for the occasion, and because two pilots were involved in the kill a second one had to be hastily prepared.

Flak again inflicted a fatality on the wing during the afternoon of 25 November when No 411 Sqn's Flg Off L G D Pow (in PV203) was hit while attacking a train near Dorsten.

No 126 Wing was very active the following day, flying 100 sorties. The results were promising, with one Fw 190 shot down, eight rail cuts made, six locomotives shot up, one of which was claimed destroyed, and several motor transports and barges strafed. The Operational Summary recalled;

'MacPherson led the last show of the day (by No 412 Sqn) and they dropped all their bombs in the target area, with many near misses around a railway bridge. It was on the way home that Flg Off F T Murray (in MT882) spotted three Fw 190s. He at first believed them to be American aircraft due to their markings, which were the same as the American roundels except that there was a black cross in the centre instead of the usual star. Flg Off Murray singled one out and it was last seen going down in flames.'

This was the last of just five aerial victories claimed by No 126 Wing in November. While German fighters had made only sporadic appearances over Holland during this period, the destruction wrought by the wing on the ground had been impressive – 62 rail cuts, six locomotives destroyed and 27 damaged and more than 100 vehicles left as 'flamers' or 'smokers' following the delivery of 2000 bombs. And incredibly, despite the appalling Dutch weather, the wing had managed to fly sorties on almost every day of the month.

1 December dawned with 'typical Netherlands weather' – ten-tenths cloud at 5000 ft all day. The following day was much the same, with the only sortie flown being a weather reconnaissance by No 412 Sqn. The 3rd saw an improvement in conditions, and operations started early in the morning. However, high winds, rain and hail brought all flying to a halt midway through the afternoon. By then No 411 Sqn's CO, Sqn Ldr E G Lapp (in TA839), and Flt Lt E T Gardner (in NH380) had claimed a Bf 109 destroyed near Venlo. This shared kill gave Lapp ace status. No 412 Sqn also spotted a few Me 262s and gave chase with no results. Considering the weather, the wing put up a good show with 102 sorties, during which 74 500-lb bombs were dropped.

Successful rail cuts would be the order of the day on 4 December, with missions being launched by all four squadrons to the Bocholt-Borken area. The end result was eight rail cuts and one locomotive and two vehicles destroyed.

The Luftwaffe made an appearance the following day, and again the wing did not hesitate to attack despite the one-sided odds. Although the 5th had got off to a slow start due to early weather delays, all four units put in a solid performance that culminated with No 412 Sqn engaging 50+ Bf 109s near Wesel at 1140 hrs. Led by Flg Off F T Murray (in PV352), the five Spitfires had initially bombed targets south of Coesfeld, before running into the enemy aircraft on their way home. Without hesitation, the Spitfire pilots tore into the enemy formation and came away with two Bf 109s shot down by future five-kill ace Flg Off Murray. Four more German fighters were claimed as probables. Flg Off C W H Glithero (in MK698) was forced to crash-land near Wachendonk, however, whereupon he was captured,

Overall, the day's totals came to 126 sorties, 231 500-lb bombs dropped, two enemy aircraft destroyed and five probables, two locomotives destroyed and one damaged and eight railway carriages destroyed.

Fog and ground mist greeted the pilots and groundcrews once again on 6 December, although all aircraft bar one managed to depart B80 Volkel and land at their new site at B88 Heesch during the course of the day. It was another display of excellent airmanship on the part of the pilots and their commanders. Wg Cdr 'Dal' Russel, after a thorough briefing, had carefully spread the flights' departures out over the afternoon, thus avoiding the possibility of mid-air collisions. The Operation Summary for the day summed it up best when it stated that 'the pilots really greased their kites in so well that there was not one mishap – and all that despite a persistent crosswind'.

All day long the wing's ground parties arrived and set up shop. The groundcrews warmly welcomed the new site, for now they had a proper floor underfoot and a roof over their heads. Indeed, conditions were better than expected. This would be the wing's home for the next four months. (*text continues on page 77*)

(*text continues on page 77*)

No 126 Wing Commander Flying Wg Cdr Blair Dalzel 'Dal' Russel was one of the most experienced pilots in the RCAF. He had served with No 1 Sqn RCAF during the Battle of Britain and would go on to command No 126 Wing from 8 July 1944 to 26 January 1945. Russel ended the war with a score of two and five shared destroyed, two probables and four damaged (*DND PL 42559*)

COLOUR PLATES

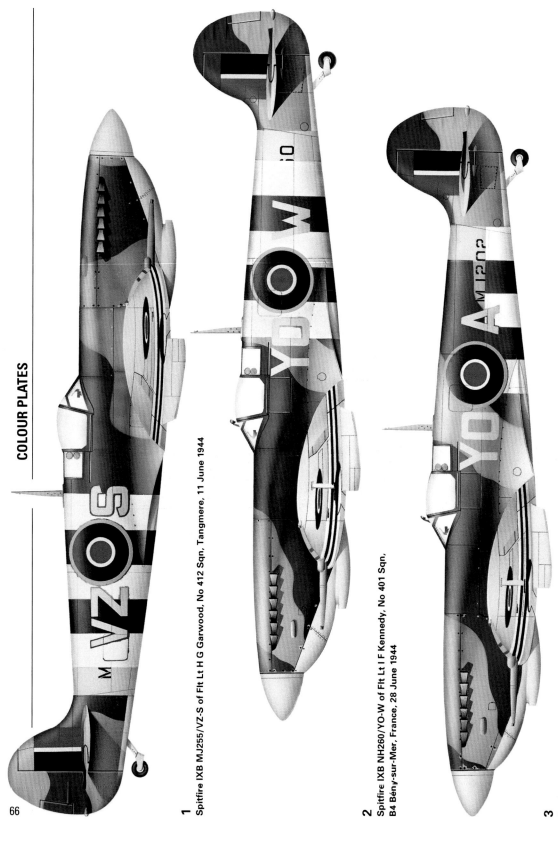

1
Spitfire IXB MJ255/VZ-S of Flt Lt H G Garwood, No 412 Sqn, Tangmere, 11 June 1944

2
Spitfire IXB NH260/YO-W of Flt Lt I F Kennedy, No 401 Sqn,
B4 Bény-sur-Mer, France, 28 June 1944

3
Spitfire IXB MJ202/YO-A of Flg Off A L Sinclair, No 401 Sqn, B68 Le Culot, Belgium, late September 1944

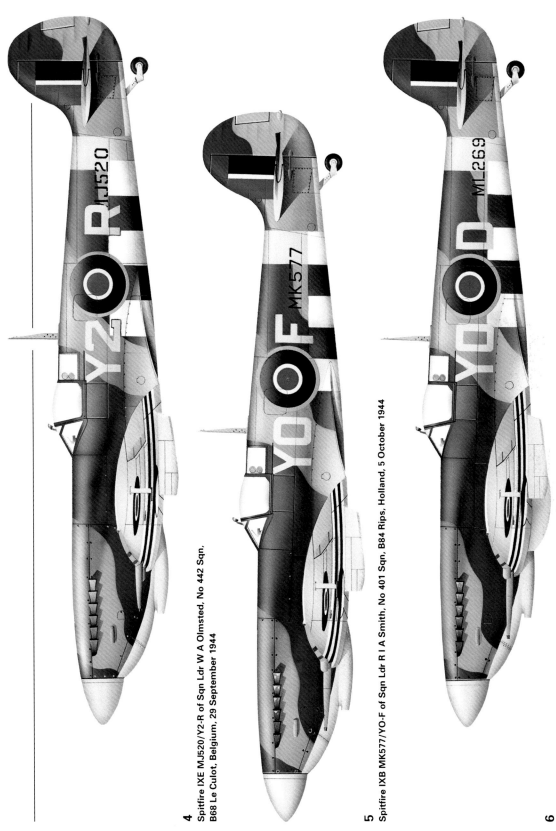

4

Spitfire IXE MJ520/Y2-R of Sqn Ldr W A Olmsted, No 442 Sqn,
B68 Le Culot, Belgium, 29 September 1944

5

Spitfire IXB MK577/YO-F of Sqn Ldr R I A Smith, No 401 Sqn, B84 Rips, Holland, 5 October 1944

6

Spitfire IXB ML269/YO-D of Flt Lt R M Davenport, No 401 Sqn, B84 Rips, Holland, 5 October 1944

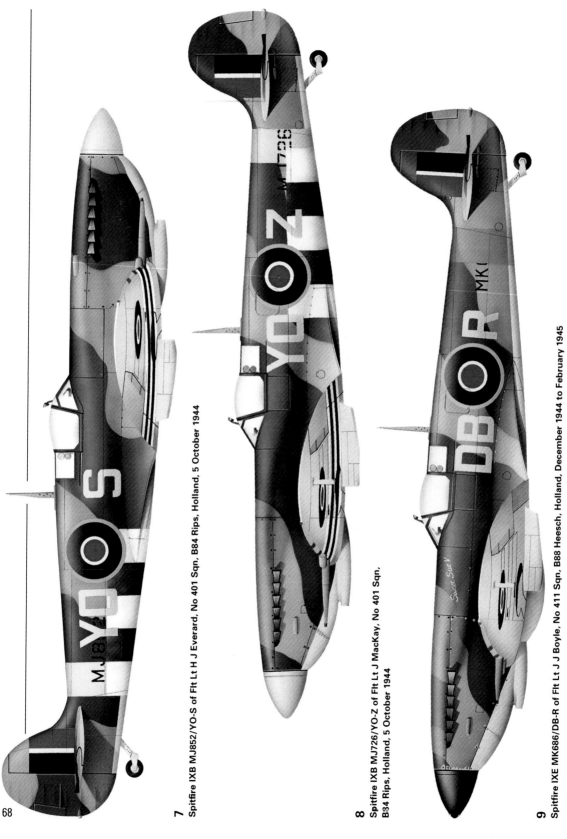

7
Spitfire IXB MJ852/YO-S of Flt Lt H J Everard, No 401 Sqn, B84 Rips, Holland, 5 October 1944

8
Spitfire IXB MJ726/YO-Z of Flt Lt J MacKay, No 401 Sqn, B34 Rips, Holland, 5 October 1944

9
Spitfire IXE MK686/DB-R of Flt Lt J J Boyle, No 411 Sqn, B88 Heesch, Holland, December 1944 to February 1945

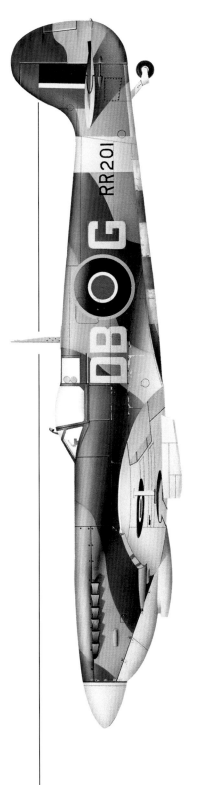

10
Spitfire IXE RR201/DB-G of Flt Lt R J Audet, No 411 Sqn,
B88 Heesch, Holland, 29 December 1944

11
Spitfire IXE MJ445/YO-A of Flg Off G D A T Cameron, No 401 Sqn, B88 Heesch, Holland, 1 January 1945

12
Spitfire IXE MK686/DB-L of Flt Lt J J Boyle, No 411 Sqn, B88 Heesch, Holland, early January 1945

13
Spitfire IXB MJ980/YO-M of Flt Lt J MacKay, No 401 Sqn, B88 Heesch, Holland, 14 January 1945

14
Spitfire IXE PT883/Y2-A of Flt Lt J E Reade, No 442 Sqn, B88 Heesch, Holland, 14 January 1945

15
Spitfire IXB ML141/YO-E of Flg Off D F Church, No 401 Sqn, B88 Heesch, Holland, 23 January 1945

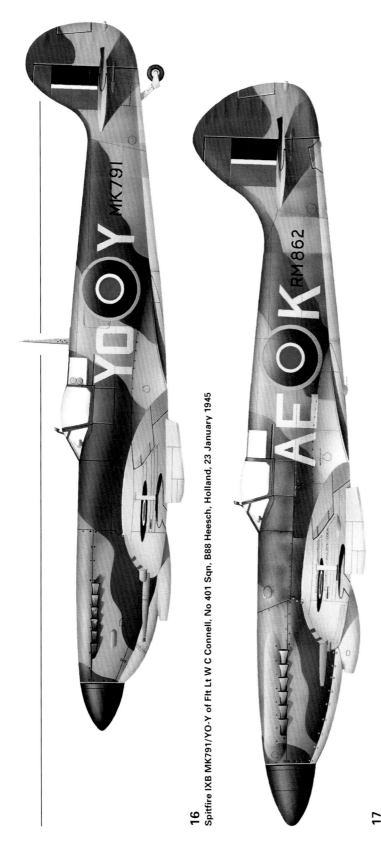

16
Spitfire IXB MK791/YO-Y of Flt Lt W C Connell, No 401 Sqn, B88 Heesch, Holland, 23 January 1945

17
Spitfire XIV RM862/AE-K of Flt Lt K S Sleep, No 402 Sqn, B88 Heesch, Holland, 25 February 1945

18
Spitfire IXB MH847/YO-N of Sqn Ldr W T Klersy, No 401 Sqn, B88 Heesch, Holland, 1 March 1945

19
Spitfire IXB MK203/YO-C of Flt Lt L N Watt, No 401 Sqn, B88 Heesch, Holland, 12 March 1945

20
Spitfire XIV RM875/AE-H of Flg Off H C Nicholson, No 402 Sqn, B88 Heesch, Holland, 13 March 1945

21
Spitfire XIV RM727/AE-P of Flt Lt H A Cowan, No 402 Sqn, B88 Heesch, Holland, 30 March 1945

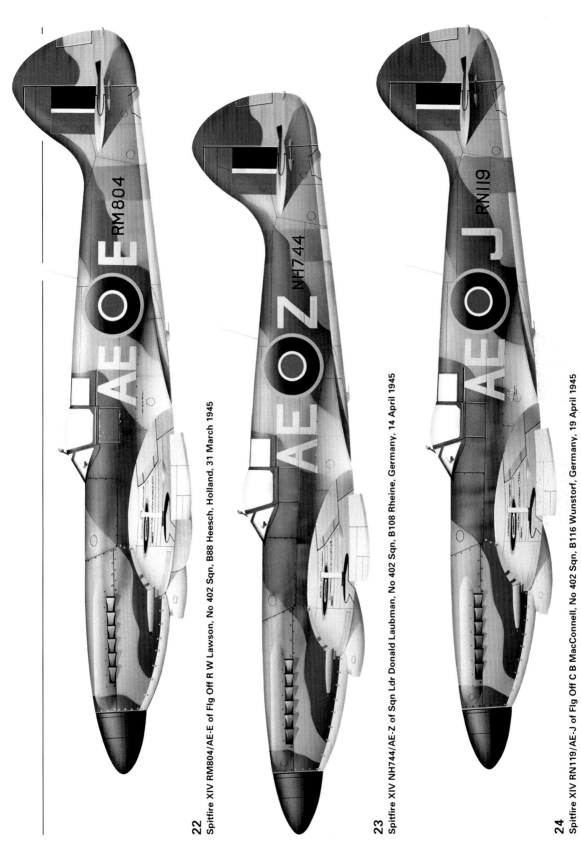

22
Spitfire XIV RM804/AE-E of Flg Off R W Lawson, No 402 Sqn, B88 Heesch, Holland, 31 March 1945

23
Spitfire XIV NH744/AE-Z of Sqn Ldr Donald Laubman, No 402 Sqn, B108 Rheine, Germany, 14 April 1945

24
Spitfire XIV RN119/AE-J of Flg Off C B MacConnell, No 402 Sqn, B116 Wunstorf, Germany, 19 April 1945

25

Spitfire IXB PL344/YO-H of Sqn Ldr W T Klersy, No 401 Sqn, B116 Wunstorf, 20 April 1945

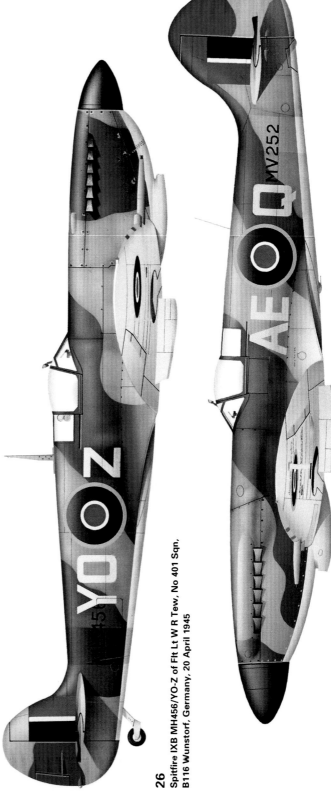

26

Spitfire IXB MH456/YO-Z of Flt Lt W R Tew, No 401 Sqn,
B116 Wunstorf, Germany, 20 April 1945

27

Spitfire XIV MV252/AE-Q of Flt Lt S M Knight, No 402 Sqn, B116 Wunstorf, Germany, 30 April 1945

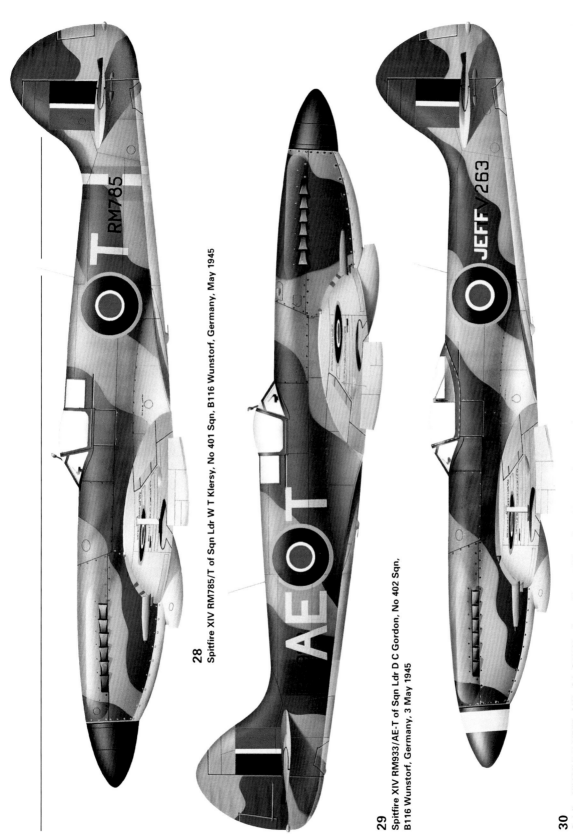

28
Spitfire XIV RM785/T of Sqn Ldr W T Klersy, No 401 Sqn, B116 Wunstorf, Germany, May 1945

29
Spitfire XIV RM933/AE-T of Sqn Ldr D C Gordon, No 402 Sqn,
B116 Wunstorf, Germany, 3 May 1945

30
Spitfire XIV MV263/JEFF of Wg Cdr G W Northcott, No 126 Wing, B174 Utersen, Germany, September 1945

1
No 401 'Ram' Squadron

2
No 402 'Winnipeg Bear' Squadron

3
No 411 'Grizzly Bear' Squadron

4
No 412 'Falcon' Squadron

No 126 Wing's contribution to the war effort came in many forms. There was the obvious bombing and shooting down of the enemy, but there was also the humanitarian side. The rain on 6 December prevented the four units from immediately commencing operations from their new strip – a single weather reconnaissance flight generated soon after their arrival confirmed the obvious. For once the pilots were not too upset about this, as the previous evening's party had left the wing feeling pretty good about itself. Reports were still coming in to B88 describing the 'magnificent party on St Nicholas Day' given by the wing for the children of Nistelrode.

About 500 children were crowded into a small schoolhouse, where they wildly greeted St Nicholas. It was announced that the party was 'made possible by St Nick's brother in Canada "who sent over five special transport aeroplanes filled with presents"'. Every man in the wing contributed to those gifts, and as a tribute to the men a choir of 40 children sang 'O Canada' in perfect English. It was a fitting end to the wing's stay at B80, and a welcome respite from the daily grind of operations.

The first missions flown from Heesch on 8 December proved eventful, with the day's Operational Summary noting that 'the programme of rail interdiction was relentlessly followed as squadron after squadron bounded into the blue to harass and punish the tired enemy'. No 401 Sqn began operations just after 0900 hrs with a dive-bombing mission northwest of Coesfeld. Early in the afternoon the marshalling yards in Rheine were attacked, the six-aircraft flight being bounced by three Me 262s that failed to score any hits. No 442 Sqn Spitfires chased three more jet fighters from Coesfeld to Groenlo, where they pulled away and disappeared into cloud.

The next day the wing was once again grounded as the day-on/day-off nature of the Dutch weather played havoc with operations. Just two sorties were flown for 'nil' results. 10 December saw the rail interdiction programme again in full swing, with the bridge over the Twente Canal finally being destroyed by No 401 Sqn after it had been targeted for several weeks. The Operational Summary recorded, 'the bridge seemed to crumple into the water, which pleased the pilots immensely, as they have been after this target for many weeks'. Prior to the bridge being destroyed 'eight Fw 190s and four Me 109s' had been spotted, and one of the latter was destroyed by Flg Off Don Church (in EN569) for the first of his three kills. Flg Off G D Cameron (in MJ386) damaged two of the

Railway workshops were among the favourite targets for medium bombers and the Typhoon wings of the 2nd TAF. While Spitfires may have damaged hundreds of locomotives, forcing them into workshops such as this one, they were readily repairable and usually back in service after a short time. However, the destruction of a repair facility dramatically slowed this process (*Public Archives of Canada PL 31981*)

Local labour was used whenever possible. Here Dutch workmen dig drainage ditches at B88 Heesch. No 412 Sqn's MJ275/VZ-J and MJ452/VZ-L stand ready with single 500-lb bombs attached. VZ-J would be used by Flt Lt J A Swan to down a Bf 109 on New Year's Day 1945. The aircraft was subsequently shot down by flak on 30 March, killing Flt Lt W J Anderson. MJ452 survived the war (*Author's Collection*)

Fw 190s. A total of 78 sorties were flown that day, and aside from the aerial successes, eight rail cuts were made and one bridge destroyed.

The next few days saw bad weather and few sorties flown. From 11 to 13 December just 59 sorties were undertaken, resulting in four rail cuts and four damaged rail cars. On the 14th the wing was back in action late in the day. Heavy fog and mist kept aircraft grounded until 1349 hrs, when a weather reconnaissance and dive-bombing mission was undertaken at the start of a very busy two to three hours for all four squadrons – they squeezed in a total of 54 sorties for fairly good results.

No 412 Sqn was the first to see action, attacking a train and a factory southeast of Bocholt. Having just knocked out a flak battery, the unit spotted Bf 109s from III./JG 26 being chased by Tempest Vs of No 56 Sqn. Joining in the hunt, Sqn Ldr J N Newall (in PT964) and Flt Lt F H Richards (in PT992) each claimed a Messerschmitt fighter destroyed. Several other pilots from the unit also had a 'grandstand seat watching several V2s on their way up into the blue'.

14 December would see No 442 Sqn CO Sqn Ldr W A Olmsted (in PV316) fly his last mission, which ended in dramatic fashion. The account from the Operational Summary read as follows;

'After outstanding leadership against ground targets, Olmsted finally completed another tour today by bailing out for the second time in six weeks. He skirted the Ruhr districts, directing all his sections of bombs accurately on a marshalling yard at Bocholt and pressing home his attack so seriously that he was apparently hit by flak without his knowledge. On the way home he was finally forced to bail out in the Grave area. Grp Capt McGregor and Wg Cdr Russel went out to bring him home, but the army beat them to it and delivered him to base safe and sound, none the worse for his experience.'

AVM Harry Broadhurst, Air Officer Commanding (AOC) No 83 Group, inspected the runway, perimeter tracks, dispersals and campsite at B88 on the afternoon of the 15th. He approved of the layout and informed the wing that on completion of the fifth dispersal area and housing, No 402 Sqn with its Spitfire XIVs would be joining the outfit from No 125 Wing – the unit eventually arrived from B64 Diest on 27 December.

The 15th was also a hectic day for No 126 Wing in the air, with all four squadrons flying the first fighter sweep in months. Wg Cdr Russel led Nos 412 and 401 Sqns to Rheine and Osnabrück, while Sqn Ldr Lapp took Nos 411 and 442 Sqns on a reciprocal course. The sweep, however, was uneventful, with only US heavy bombers, Mustangs, Thunderbolts and Lightnings spotted during the whole show.

The most dramatic target of the day was found on the ground by No 411 Sqn when its pilots bombed a train of 40 or 50 cars at a junction north of Dorsten. One well-placed 500-lb weapon found its mark, hitting a rail car full of ammunition. The resulting explosion started a fire that created a huge column of smoke rising to 6000 ft. Smaller explosions followed, with streams of tracers flying through the air. Fifteen rail cars were destroyed outright. The day ended with 117 sorties having been flown and 65 500-lbs bombs dropped for 13 rail cuts, 24 rail cars destroyed and one road/rail bridge demolished.

Dawn on 16 December revealed that the 'weather was so duff' the only mission of the day was forced to return before it reached Nijmegen. Persistent low cloud resulted in the wing being released at 1500 hrs. The quiet experienced at B88 was in sharp contrast to what was happening hundreds of miles south in the American section of the frontlines. While the 'duff' weather was a great hindrance to Allied air operations, it was a critical asset for German plans in the Ardennes.

In the early morning hours of the 16th, the Germans launched Operation *Wacht am Rhein* ('Watch on the Rhine'). Seven Panzer divisions and thirteen infantry divisions pushed through American lines in the Ardennes Forest in Luxembourg. Hitler's ultimate goal for his offensive was to capture the strategic port of Antwerp, as well as Brussels and Namur. While the Germans made early gains and the weather kept the tactical air forces grounded, it was only a matter of time before the Allied line would stiffen and stop the enemy before it reached its objectives. And amazingly, while the Wehrmacht had managed to assemble, move and supply this large Panzer force, the Luftwaffe had also undergone an extraordinary metamorphosis.

The losses suffered by the Jagdwaffe during D-Day and the Battle for Normandy had, for all intents and purposes, destroyed its ability to gain even local air

No 411 Sqn's PL320/DB-R provides the backdrop for this snapshot of LAC J Macauley. PL320 served with No 132 Sqn from 20 July 1944 until it was transferred to No 411 Sqn on 9 September. Passed on to No 412 Sqn on 5 April 1945, the fighter was later sold to Turkey in June 1947 (*Public Archives of Canada PL 320*)

superiority for short periods of time. For much of the autumn the Jagdwaffe had been absent over the battlefield. This was due in large part to the weather and the ongoing battles with the US Eighth Air Force over Germany. But by mid-December the numbers had changed. Production of fighter aircraft during the autumn months had increased, and new models like the Fw 190D and Bf 109K were reaching the frontline in large numbers. By mid-November the Germans had 3300 fighters in the West. It was an incredible achievement.

However, while these numbers were impressive, the Luftwaffe had failed in one critical area – pilot training. The men available to fly these machines were either newly trained pilots (who could barely keep their aircraft in the air) or ex-bomber and transport crews who were not trained for fighter combat. Fuel shortages meant that new pilots were restricted to just a few hours of flying time each prior to arriving in the frontline, and this made them easy targets for well trained Allied pilots.

And while the Wehrmacht's offensive had taken the Allied armies by surprise, the Luftwaffe was planning its own 'Big Blow'.

No 126 Wing's location meant that it had no chance of having a direct impact on the new German offensive, but that did not preclude it from contributing in its own way. A foreshadowing of what the Jagdwaffe had in store for the Allies happened on the morning of the 17th when eight enemy aircraft flew 'balls out' at 2000 ft over the airfield. Weather again restricted flying, and only 15 sorties were flown. No 411 Sqn also welcomed its new CO, Sqn Ldr J N Newell, on this date. Northern Irishman Newell took over from Sqn Ldr E G Lapp, who had now completed his second tour. Lapp's departure marked a complete turnover of pilots in the unit since D-Day.

On 18 December the Luftwaffe returned when two Me 262s tore across the field at about 500 ft, providing everyone with their 'big thrill' for the day. Four aircraft on immediate readiness took off after them, but the jets disappeared too quickly 'for any joy'. In an effort to support the beleaguered American troops in the Ardennes, Nos 412 and 442 Sqns, led by Wg Cdr Russel, flew a sweep in the Aachen area but found no targets to attack.

No 411 Sqn pilots ham it up for the camera in the autumn of 1944. Kneeling is Flt Lt J J Boyle, with Sqn Ldr J N Newell immediately behind him and Flt Lt E G Ireland to his left. The identity of the pilot to the right enthusiastically recalling a recent dogfight is unknown. Newell would lead No 411 Sqn from 19 December 1944 through to 25 June 1945 (*DND PMR 78-56*)

Increasing ground haze the following day shortened the flying programme, but not before the wing had performed three two-squadron sweeps in the Dusseldorf and Paderborn areas. The Operational Summary concluded the day on a rather optimistic note;

'Nothing of note was seen but the purpose of intimidating the Huns may have been achieved for none were reported, even though we were directly over their bases.'

For the next three days the wing was grounded due to more poor

In the Canadian Archives this photograph is captioned as 'flak damage in Holland, 1944'. It was actually a fragmentation bomb dropped by a German hit-and-run raider that caused the damage to this No 126 Wing Spitfire at B80, however. The 'all clear' following the raid has yet to be given as both groundcrew are still wearing their tin helmets (*Public Archives of Canada PL 33414*)

weather. Continuing reports of enemy air activity during this period kept the Spitfire units focused and ready for action. Even with heavy ground haze persisting through the morning of the 23rd, some patrols and three sweeps were flown in the afternoon for a surprising total of 66 sorties. First up was No 401 Sqn, with no results. No 411 Sqn sortied next, performing a 12-aircraft sweep/armed reconnaissance to investigate Wahn airfield between Bonn and Cologne. No aircraft were seen on the base or in the air, but on the way home two Me 262s were encountered just east of Eindhoven. Flt Lt J J Boyle (in TA858) managed to damage one of the jets for the only claim of the day.

Luftwaffe activity was on the increase, and as 24 December dawned clear and crisp, No 126 Wing would encounter 'many Huns' but only No 412 Sqn would score. Both it and No 442 Sqn departed on the first sweep of the day at 0847 hrs to the Neuss/Duren area. It again proved to be uneventful, but this was followed by another sweep in the same area by No 412 Sqn at 1225 hrs. This time Allied radar control vectored the unit onto 45+ Fw 190s south of Julich, the Spitfires using their height advantage to immediately bounce the enemy fighters. Flt Lt C W Fox (in PT964) and future ace Flt Lt M D Boyd (in PL402) each destroyed an Fw 190, while Sqn Ldr D H Dover (in PV234) claimed two damaged and Flt Lt R N Earle (in PK998) damaged a third fighter.

At this point in the offensive it seems that the 'rail interdiction programme' was put on hold as dive-bombing missions were replaced with sweeps and armed reconnaissance sorties – 17 December was the last day that the wing dropped any bombs.

Christmas Day dawned with a heavy programme of operations that would result in great excitement, and pride, for the wing. No 411 Sqn had flown the first sweep at 1125 hrs, and as the unit's Flt Lt Jack Boyle (in MK686) and his wingman returned early due to mechanical problems they spotted an Me 262 from II./KG 51 almost directly overhead B88. The men on the ground reacted quickly to the spectacle in the air. As they waited in line for their noon Christmas dinner, 'the long queue of airmen bit the dust when an Me 262 was clobbered by the cannon fire of Flt Lt Jack Boyle'. It was also an exhilarating experience for the watching groundcrew too, as they had finally got to see, close up, exactly what their aircraft and pilots did when fighting the Luftwaffe. The Operational Summary recorded;

'Jack set the port jet unit on fire and then got many other strikes in three more bursts. The enemy aircraft tried to crash-land but clipped the trees and then exploded mightily as it hit the ground. The disintegration was so great that the RAF Regiment subsequently had trouble locating the bits and pieces.'

After the war Jack Boyle described the events on that day as he saw them;

'Our entire wing received orders to provide maximum air support in the American sector to the south, where the German army had broken through our lines in what came to be known as the Battle of the Bulge. Our excitement was running high as we were briefed on the extensive German fighter activity around Bastogne, having first been told that our entire wing would be taking off within the hour. No 411 Sqn was the last to go, and it wasn't too long before we could hear the R/T chatter of those ahead reporting enemy sightings. Our sense of anticipation grew by leaps and bounds.

'In the midst of this, I couldn't believe my ears when I heard my new No 2 calling to report a ropy engine that was running so rough he thought he shouldn't go on. Since a lame aircraft was never permitted to go home alone, this meant that I would have to escort him back to base and miss out on all the activity going on just ahead of us. I decided that we couldn't risk going on and reported to the CO that we were heading for home. I was sorely disappointed by this turn of events, and grumbled to myself all the way home.

'As were neared Heesch, we were far too high to land, so in an irritable mood, and to get rid of excess height as quickly as possible, I stuck the nose of my fighter almost straight down in a screaming spiral dive. As my speed shot well past the maximum permissible, out of nowhere appeared an Me 262 jet. It took only a second to activate my gunsight and release my guns' safety switch, and then I was right behind him. My first burst of cannon fire hit his port engine pod and it began streaming dense smoke. He immediately dove for the deck as an evasive tactic, but with only one engine he couldn't outrun me. I scored several more hits before he clipped some tall trees and then hit the ground at an almost flat angle. His aircraft disintegrated in stages from nose to tail, ripping up the turf as it cart-wheeled in a trail of smoke and flame. As I circled, Dutch farmers emerged from the barns and waved up to me.'

Shortly after Boyle had claimed his rare Me 262 kill, 13 Spitfires from No 401 Sqn encountered Bf 109s from *Stab* JG 77 near Euskirchen. Flt Lt John MacKay (in MJ980) shot down one of the German fighters, and a second was shared by Flt Lt W C Connell (in MK791) and Flt Sgt A K Woodill (in MH761). The unit did not escape from this clash unscathed, however, as its CO, Sqn Ldr H J Everard (in MJ852), was forced to bail out south of Venlo when his Spitfire was hit by debris from one of the Bf 109s. He spent

The official caption for this photograph states that the pilot standing rather sheepishly alongside this crumpled No 411 Sqn Spitfire is Flg Off E D Kelly. The aircraft purportedly swung on take-off and shed both wings at B88 Heesch in December 1944. However, there is no record of the unit losing an aircraft in such a crash during that month, while Flg Off E D Kelly was actually assigned to No 412 Sqn – he had previously served with No 403 Sqn! Regardless of who this is, and when the accident happened, this shot perfectly illustrates the sheer variety of hazards facing pilots in the frontline in 1944-45, combat being just being one of them. In order to give its pilots a break from the dangers of operations, the RCAF rotated its Spitfire pilots after 200 hours of combat flying (*Public Archives of Canada PMR 78-460*)

the rest of the conflict as a PoW, high-scoring ace Sqn Ldr Bill Klersy taking his place at the head of No 401 Sqn.

No 411 Sqn again encountered the elusive German jet on 26 December when, during its second sweep of the day, Flt Lt E G Ireland (in PL430) damaged one over Geilenkirchen. His claim brought the unit's score to 'one jet job destroyed and two damaged in three consecutive days. This, to the best of our knowledge, puts the squadron in the lead as jet job killers, with Flt Lt Boyle being the jet-job king'. These results did indeed give No 126 Wing the lead in the 2nd TAF when it came to destroying or damaging enemy jets.

To round out the day, Nos 401 and 412 Sqns flew a rare escort mission for 150 Lancasters sent to bomb St Vith, the units providing a 'target cover job'.

Despite ground haze restricting operations to a brief window from 1000 hrs through to 1600 hrs on the 27th, the wing succeeded in downing four Bf 109s and damaging another Me 262 – the latter, engaged near Aachen, was credited to No 442 Sqn's Flg Off M A Perkins (in PT883). At 1110 hrs aircraft from No 411 Sqn spotted Bf 109s fighting USAAF fighters over Malmedy-St Vith and the Canadian pilots joined the fray. Flt Lts E G Ireland (in PL430) and R M Cook (in NH380) each claimed one apiece, as did Flg Off M G Graham (in MK788). A short while later No 412 Sqn was attacked by three Bf 109s over Rheine airfield, one of which was destroyed by Flt Lt C W Fox (in PT535).

27 December also saw the arrival of No 402 Sqn and its complement of Spitfire XIVs from No 125 Wing at B64 Diest, in Belgium.

No 126 Wing's Christmas Day accomplishments did not go unnoticed, for on 28 December AVM Broadhurst congratulated the wing with a signal praising its efforts. 'All personnel very deeply

No 402 Sqn's Spitfire XIV RM625 shortly before it joined No 126 Wing on 27 December 1944. The unit was part of No 125 Wing at B64 Diest, in Belgium, from 1 November until 26 December. RM625 served with both Nos 91 and 402 Sqns, and was eventually sold to the Belgium Air Force in 1948 (*No 402 Sqn Archives*)

Many fighter pilots and historians alike considered the Griffon-engined Spitfire XIV to be the best piston-engined single-seat fighter of the war, and the best of all the Spitfire variants to see action in this conflict. Its powerful 2050 hp engine and its massive five-bladed propeller gave it a top speed of 439 mph at 24,500 ft. In tactical trials the Mk XIV was clearly superior when compared to early versions of the Fw 190A and Bf 109G. Reports from the Air Fighting Development Unit stated;

COMBAT TRIAL AGAINST Fw 190

Maximum speeds
From 0 ft to 5000 ft and 15,000 ft to 20,000 ft, the Spitfire XIV is only 20 mph faster. At all other heights it is up to 60 mph faster than the Fw 190 (BMW 801D). It is estimated to have about the same maximum speed as the new Fw 190D (DB 603) at all heights.

Maximum climb
The Spitfire XIV has a considerably greater rate of climb than the Fw 190 (BMW 801D) or (estimated) the Fw 190D (DB 603) at all heights.

Dive
After the initial part of the dive, during which the Fw 190 gains slightly, the Spitfire XIV has a slight advantage.

Turning circle
The Spitfire XIV can easily turn inside the Fw 190, though in the case of a right hand turn this difference is not quite so pronounced.

Rate of roll
The Fw 190 is very much better.

Conclusions
In defence, the Spitfire XIV should use its remarkable rate of climb and superior turning circle against any enemy aircraft. In the attack it can afford to mix it, but the pilot should be aware of the Fw 190's quick roll and dive. If this manoeuvre is used by the enemy in an attempt to break combat, and the Spitfire XIV follows, it will be able to close range until the Fw 190 has pulled out of its dive.

Against the Bf 109G, 'the Spitfire was superior to the Me 109G in every respect'. Compared to the Spitfire Mk IX, the Mk XIV was 'found to have better all round performance at all heights. In level flight, it is 25-35 mph faster, and has a correspondingly greater rate of climb. Its manoeuvrability is as good as a Spitfire IX. It is easy to fly, but should be handled with care when taxying and taking off. The Spitfire XIV has the best all round performance of any present-day fighter, apart from range'.

As the report clearly noted, like all the Spitfires before it, the Mk XIV's range was extremely short. And when fitted with a 90-gallon slipper tank, about 20 mph was knocked off the fighter's maximum speed.

Remarkably, only seven squadrons would be equipped with this superb fighter (three being from the RCAF, namely Nos 402, 414 and 430 Sqns) to serve in the 2nd TAF. Just 957 Mk XIVs were built in what proved to the last substantial production run of any Spitfire type.

appreciated the AOC's signal of congratulations on the work carried out on XMAS Day', part of which read as follows;

'Please convey my congratulations and thanks to all ranks for your magnificent efforts against the Hun on Christmas Day. During my visits to the wing I was most impressed with the splendid balance which was held between the requirements of operations and the festivities of the season. We are working under difficult conditions in a major battle. Therefore, your achievements are all the more creditable, and are calling forth admiration from the American Army and Air Forces.'

The praise was well deserved as the wing once again battled foul weather to mount 41 sorties on the 28th. No 401 Sqn led the way with a very fruitful sweep/armed reconnaissance mission to the Rheine-Münster area. Five locomotives were damaged along with 19 rail cars. No 411 Sqn would add one locomotive destroyed, three damaged and 18 goods trucks damaged, along with one flak wagon 'blown to Kingdom Come'.

By 29 December No 126 Wing's overall tally of aerial kills since D-Day was approaching the 200 mark, the Operational Summary noting that 'We had modestly hoped to reach that figure by the New Year'. A day of intense aerial action would see that marker easily passed. The first victory was claimed by No 411 Sqn's Flg Off R A Gilberstad (in MK686) during a sweep of Rheine at 1040 hrs. Having damaged an Fw 190, he was then attacked by two more, causing him to dive. When Gilberstad aggressively pulled out of this manoeuvre 'so adroitly at 1000 ft, his pursuer stalled, flicked and spun right into the ground'.

At midday No 401 Sqn took off on a sweep and armed reconnaissance, and at 1240 hrs the unit was bounced by the Fw 190Ds of 12./JG 54. The Canadians had Flt Lt E B Sheehy (in MK300) killed in this first pass, although future aces Flg Offs G D A T Cameron (in MJ386) and F T Murray (in MJ851) quickly exacted their revenge for their fallen comrade by downing a single 'long-nose' Fw 190D each.

The final successes of the day were claimed by pilots from No 411 Sqn one hour later when the unit, led by Sqn Ldr Newell, was vectored onto Fw 190s from 9./JG 54 near Rheine at 1335 hrs. Three fighters were initially engaged, and two of these aircraft were shot down by Flt Lts E G Ireland (in PL430) and R M Cook (in NH380). Twelve more German fighters were then seen near Osnabrück, one of which fell to Flg Off R C McCracken (in MK788) and no fewer than five (three Fw 190s and two Bf 109s) to Flt Lt R J Audet (in RR201).

According to the Operational Summary, earlier in the mission Audet, with his 'remarkable eyesight, spotted nine locomotives and a substantial number of rail cars. The results were four locos destroyed and five damaged, along with 39 rail cars. One locomotive blew up so completely that it set a nearby building on fire'. After this attack Audet spied 12 enemy aircraft near Osnabrück and quickly led his section of six aircraft into battle. There, they spotted 12 Fw 190s and Bf 109s below them. The fight was over very quickly. 'The dream of this war became a reality when Flt Lt Audet led "Yellow Section" over Osnabrück and promptly polished off five of them'. Audet was so shocked by his own prowess he only claimed four destroyed,

Opposite left
Running up at its Belgian base in early 1945, RM683/AE-N of No 402 Sqn was used by Flt Lt D Sherk to destroy an Fw 190 near Aachen on Christmas Day 1944. It remained with the squadron into the spring, when it was occasionally flown by the unit's ace CO, Sqn Ldr Don Laubman (*Author's Collection*)

Opposite right
The Spitfire XIV equipped just seven squadrons in the 2nd TAF, three of which were Canadian – Nos 402, 414 and 430 Sqns. Newly transferred from England, these No 402 Sqn Mk XIVs bask in the sun on an airfield in Holland in the late spring of 1945 (*DND PL 33035*)

No 411 Sqn pilots compare notes after the amazing 29 December 1945 missions. They are, from left to right, Flt Lt R J Audet, WO J A Kerr and Flg Offs R M Cook and Olsen. The two individuals to right are unidentified (*Public Archives of Canada PMR 78-252*)

No 411 Sqn's Flg Offs A G McNiece and Flg Off B A McPhail and Flt Lt R J Audet smile for the camera in late 1944. While based at Volkel, No 126 Wing was closer to the front than any other Allied formation. When the pilots were not flying they were being 'genned up' with geography and aircraft recognition tests (*Public Archives of Canada PMR 78-249*)

although he mentioned five successful combats. He was later awarded the fifth.

French Canadian Dick Audet had gained his wings in October 1942 and then been sent to England, where he briefly joined No 421 Sqn prior to spending much of 1943-44 with No 691 Sqn (formerly No 1623 Flight) – an anti-aircraft cooperation unit based at RAF Roborough, in Devon, that was principally tasked with towing banner targets. These humdrum tasks allowed Audet to build up a large number of flying hours in Barracudas, Defiants and Hurricanes and gain considerable experience in aircraft handling. In September 1944 he was posted to No 411 Sqn, and he became a flight commander the following month. By late December Audet had flown 52 operational sorties, and although he had made numerous attacks on ground targets, he had never seen an enemy aircraft before the afternoon of the 28th! His combat report for this amazing encounter read as follows;

'The enemy were four Me 109s and eight Fw 190s, flying line astern. I attacked an Me 109, the last aircraft in the formation. At 200 yards I opened fire, and saw strikes all over the fuselage and wing roots. The Me 109 quickly burst into flames and was seen to trail black smoke. I now went around in a defensive circle until I spotted an Fw 190. I attacked from 250 yards down to 100 yards, and from 30 degrees from line astern. I saw strikes over the cockpit and to the rear of the fuselage. It burst into flames. I saw the pilot slumped in his cockpit.

'Ahead was an Me 109 going down in a slight dive. It pulled up sharply into a climb and the cockpit canopy flew off. I gave a short burst at about 300 yards and the aircraft whipped down in a dive.

The pilot attempted to bail out, but his 'chute was ripped to shreds. I saw the Me 109 hit the ground and smash into flaming pieces.

'I next spotted an Fw 190 being pursued by a Spitfire pursued in turn by another Fw 190. I called this pilot – one from my "Yellow Section" – to break, and attacked the Me 109 from the rear. We went down in a steep dive. I opened fire at 250 yards and it burst into flames. I saw it go into the ground and burn.

'Several minutes later, while attempting to re-form my section, I spotted an Fw 190 at about 2000 ft. I dived on him and he turned into me from the right. He then flipped around in a left-hand turn and attempted a head-on attack. I slowed down to wait for him to fly into range. At about 200 yards I gave a short burst. I could not see any strikes, but he flicked violently and continued to do so until he crashed.'

Audet had made good use of his new GM2 gyro gunsight during the action, and his achievement – five enemy fighters downed in just ten minutes – was witnessed by other pilots in his squadron, and confirmed independently by analysis of his combat camera film.

Audet's air-to-air virtuosity would continue into January 1945, when he claimed a further five victories and shared in a sixth. To add to his impressive score, his last victory would be over an Me 262 on 23 January. He also damaged a second one in the same action and claimed a third jet fighter destroyed on the ground. For his efforts Audet was awarded a DFC in February followed by a Bar in March. Sadly, he was killed by flak while strafing a train on 3 March 1945.

30 December saw no flying whatsoever because of thick ground fog and low cloud, but clearer conditions the following day would allow No 126 Wing to end the year on a high note by claiming six aircraft and a V1(!) destroyed. The wing also had a pilot killed when Flt Lt R N Earle (in PT964) of No 412 Sqn crashed while attacking mechanised transport near Enschede at 1140 hrs. Five minutes later No 411 Sqn's Flt Lt J J Boyle (in TA839) destroyed a rare Ju 88 southeast of Rheine. Squadronmate, and fellow future ace, Flg Off M G Graham (in MK788) then downed a lone Fw 190D that had attempted to bounce his section in the same area. At 1210 hrs No 442 Sqn was returning from an armed reconnaissance when 15+ Bf 109s were intercepted south of Münster. Four were shot down, with single victories being claimed by Flt Lt R C Smith (in RR196) and Flg Offs G J Doyle (in PL370) and G H Watkin (in MJ283). The fourth fighter was shared by future ace Flt Lt D M Pieri (in MJ463) and Flg Off M A Perkins (NH591).

The one and only V1 'buzz bomb' shot down by the wing fell on this day too when No 401 Sqn's WO M Thomas, 'who doesn't like V1s flying in our circuit, gave one adventurous "buzz bomb" a couple of short bursts and brought it down a couple of miles southwest of our strip'.

On New Year's Eve No 126 Wing tallied its score. For the month of December its squadrons had destroyed a V1 and 32 aircraft, with 3 probables and 17 damaged. This put the wing's overall tally well beyond the 200 mark since D-Day. It was now the top-scoring wing in the 2nd TAF – a remarkable achievement, and one that would have not been possible without the tireless work of the groundcrews involved.

A close up of the new GM2 gyro gunsight fitted to the Spitfire from late 1944. A major step forward in air-to-air gunnery, the gunsight gave the 'average' fighter pilot a much better chance of scoring hits and making kills. It was used to good effect when the pilots of No 401 Sqn shot down the first Me 262 on 5 October 1944, and Flt Lt Dick Audet also praised the GM2 after he claimed his five victories in just a matter of minutes on 29 December (*Author's Collection*)

BODENPLATTE AND MARCH ON THE RHEINE

D uring the Wehrmacht's build up of forces for the Ardennes offensive the Luftwaffe was also busy assembling a formidable fighting force of 2460 aircraft, 1770 of which were single-seat fighters. It is believed that these aircraft were originally to have been used in support of the troops on the ground. However, just as the poor winter weather in late December had kept the Allied Tactical Air Forces firmly on the ground, it had prevented the Luftwaffe from bringing its aircraft to bear in any meaningful way during the battle.

Since D-Day, the Allies had enjoyed such a level of aerial superiority that the German response had been both weak and ineffective. It was now time for the Luftwaffe to strike back with everything it had. And as with the Ardennes offensive two weeks earlier, the Allies were caught by surprise.

Shortly after dawn on 1 January 1945 the Luftwaffe unleashed 986 single-seat fighters, including 24 Me 262s (as well as six Ar 234B jet bombers) against Allied tactical airfields in Operation *Bodenplatte* ('Baseplate'). While the attack was a surprise, the Allies were not caught totally unawares. A considerable number of 2nd TAF and US Ninth Air Force aircraft were already in the air conducting routine early morning patrols, and they quickly began to engage the incoming formations.

The first airfield to be hit was B78 Eindhoven, effectively targeted by JG 3. No 143 Wing, equipped with Typhoons, had two aircraft destroyed and four badly damaged, while No 30 (Reconnaissance) Wing's No 400 Sqn lost five Spitfire PR XIs and No 430 Sqn three of its new Spitfire FR XIVs and two Mustang Is.

The German fighters were next seen passing overhead B88 at 0915 hrs as they headed for airfields on their target list – Heesch was not on the latter, despite it being the closest airfield to the frontlines. Unfortunately for the Luftwaffe both Nos 411 and 442 Sqns were

No 411 Sqn Spitfires warm up their engines before departing on another mission in January 1945. The new GM2 gyro gunsight, seen here silhouetted against the windscreen of MJ334, was larger than its predecessor and restricted forward visibility. Many aces were far from enamoured with it, having already mastered the art of air-to-air gunnery and deflection shooting. For the average pilot, however, it would double the effectiveness of their air-to-air gunnery. Having previously served with both Nos 412 and 443 Sqns, MJ334 joined No 411 Sqn in late 1944 and was written off in a crash-landing at B116 on 20 April 1945 after the veteran fighter suffered inflight engine failure (*Public Archives of Canada PA 115094*)

In full fighter pilot pose, Flt Lt Norman A Keene joined No 442 Sqn from No 411 Sqn in November 1944. His only confirmed kill occurred on 1 January 1945 during the *Bodenplatte* attack on Allied airfields. Keene is a fine example of the vast majority of pilots who did not make ace, but whose contribution was nevertheless vital in achieving No 126 Wing's overall success in World War 2 (*Public Archives of Canada*)

already airborne on a fighter sweep, and just as No 401 Sqn was waiting to take off some 40 Bf 109s and Fw 190s flew overhead. The Canadian pilots gunned their engines and gave chase, followed quickly by No 412 Sqn.

Ten minutes later, Flt Lt G D A T Cameron (in MJ445) returned to base out of ammunition after claiming three Bf 109s destroyed. Squadronmate and fellow future ace Flt Lt Johnny MacKay (in MH240) came back with a handful of kills, the Operational Summary noting that 'after using most of his ammo to destroy one Hun, he emptied the balance into a second a short while after, but seeing no results closed in and flew him into the deck. He closed in on a third at very low level and repeated the same procedure, thus making three destroyed – two Fw 190s and an Me 109 – for himself'.

No 412 Sqn also caught up with the marauding German fighters, spotting 30 Bf 109s over the Venlo area and claiming four of them shot down. Flt Lt B E MacPherson (in PT186) and Flg Off V Smith claimed one each, and Sqn Ldr D H Dover (in MK306) and Flg Off E D Kelly (in PT352) shared a third.

No 411 Sqn's Flt Lt Dick Audet (in PL493) spotted two Fw 190s over the Twente area and quickly shot them down. The final victories claimed against the first wave of attacking aircraft fell to No 442 Sqn, whose pilots began returning to B88 from their sweep just in time to engage the enemy. Due to a problem with his drop tank Flt Lt R C Smith had headed for home early, and on his way back he heard that enemy fighters were over Eindhoven. The Operational Summary noted, 'He therefore found himself to be the lone Allied aircraft amongst two-score or more enemy aircraft'. Forgetting the rule about flying alone, Smith attacked the fighters over the town and shot down a Bf 109 and damaged a second. To add to the drama he ran out of fuel at 7000 ft, but was able to make a perfect dead stick landing.

Squadronmate Flt Lt Don Gordon (in MH728) was also returning early when he spotted fighters near Heesch. Having downed two Fw 190s, both he and his fighter were then hit by Allied AA and he crash-landed south of the airfield. The rest of No 442 Sqn ran into enemy fighters west of Venlo, where Flt Lt D M Pieri (in NH489) claimed two Fw 190s shot down and two damaged and Flt Lt N A Keene (MJ425) one Focke-Wulf destroyed. The unit also suffered No 126 Wing's first fatality of the day during this clash when Flg Off D A Brigden (in MK420) was shot down by enemy fighters.

With its aircraft refuelled and rearmed, No 412 Sqn was sent aloft again on an armed reconnaissance mission shortly after 1100 hrs. During the course of the patrol Flt Lt W J Banks (in ML277) shot down a lone Ju 88 south of Hamm – this was his ninth, and last, kill. At 1525 hrs No 401 Sqn attacked Rheine airfield on a 'Rat Hunt' in search of Me 262s. Although none were found, three Bf 109s were shot down by Flt Lt J C Lee (in ML141), Flg Off D F Church (in MK888) and Plt Off D M Horsburgh (EN569).

The wing's final victories came 30 minutes later when pilots from No 412 Sqn – on their third mission of the day – spotted two Bf 109s southeast of Osnabrück. Sqn Ldr D H Dover (in PV234) destroyed one and Flt Lt J A Swan (in MJ275) was credited with the second.

Unfortunately, an unseen Bf 109 also joined the fray and shot down Flt Lt J P Doak (in MJ877) near Gutersloh. He perished in the crash.

Operation *Bodenplatte* had been a complete failure as the Luftwaffe had fallen far short of destroying the 400-500 Allied aircraft that it had hoped for. While the damage inflicted had in some cases been serious, most of the Allied aircraft lost (as many as 300) were non-operational types. At most, five 2nd TAF squadrons were temporarily grounded until their losses could be made good. Luftwaffe losses, on the other hand, had been shattering – 271 fighters shot down and 65 damaged, 143 pilots dead or missing, 70 taken prisoner and 21 wounded.

Not only were Allied pilots victorious, ground-based AA fire had contributed greatly with 97 aircraft claimed to have been shot down. Even before the German fighters had reached Allied lines they had had to run the gauntlet of their own flak defences. All German flak units were usually warned of the Luftwaffe sorties planned for each day, but on 1 January, in order to keep the raid secret, they were not informed. Unused to seeing so many German aircraft in the air at the same time, the gunners assumed that they were Allied fighter-bombers and duly inflicted grievous losses on the Jagdwaffe.

Allied fighters shot down somewhere between 65 and 80 German aircraft, with No 126 Wing's contribution for the day being an impressive 24 kills – a new record for a single day of air combat. The previous record had been 22 on 27 September 1944. The only unit within the wing not to score that day was No 402 Sqn, which was only able to put up two-man flights due to a scarcity of serviceable Griffon-powered Spitfires.

The attack had been intense, but brief, and as soon as the raiders disappeared normal operations resumed for everyone involved. No 126 Wing had been spared the destruction meted out to several other wings, and now it was time to add up the numbers. The wing had flown 141 sorties during the course of the day. No 401 Sqn had been credited with nine enemy fighters destroyed, one probably destroyed, one damaged and one Me 262 damaged. No 412 Sqn had downed six enemy fighters and one Ju 88, No 442 Sqn claimed six destroyed, two probably destroyed and one Me 262 damaged, and No 411 Sqn tallied two victories, both to Flt Lt Audet.

While the New Year had come in with a bang, 2 January was very much an anti-climax with just 16 sorties flown. It was also a day spent getting serviceability improved and typing and signing countless Combat Reports.

What the Germans could not do with their New Year's day attack weather did for the month of January. The onset of snow storms virtually closed B88, and there were just four days in the month when enemy aircraft were engaged. Ground targets, of course, continued to be shot up, but there too the levels of success achieved were limited. It would be the month where 'duff weather again held 126 on the ground'.

4 January proved, however, to be one of the exceptions. The Operational Summary reported that 'The day started as though it would be clampers again, but weather lifted somewhat just around noon'. No 411 Sqn managed to 'squeeze in two shows for the day, with

the first bearing the most fruit'. Airborne at 1318 hrs, the unit soon sighted seven Fw 190s (possibly from I./JG 1) in the Hengelo area. The resulting clash was very one-sided, with six enemy aircraft destroyed for the loss of Flg Off K J Thomson (in RK810) – he bailed out and was captured. Flg Off M G Graham (in MK788) led the way with two kills to give him ace status, while Flt Lt R J Audet (in PV347) claimed one and one shared with future ace Flt Lt J J Boyle (in PL430). Boyle also bagged an Fw 190 by himself, as did Flt Lt H D Carr (in PL433).

The following day dawned with good flying weather, and the wing generated the most sorties in a single day for the entire month – 180. The results, however, were meagre. Fighter sweeps and armed reconnaissance were flown in the Lingen/Rheine/Osnabrück/Münster areas, but by the end of the day just five locomotives had been destroyed.

The next four days brought weather that was definitely 'Pro-Nazi', with snowstorms on the 8th preventing even weather reconnaissance flights from being flown. The Operational Summary noted, 'Late afternoon saw some 50+ pilots getting some real exercise for a change wielding shovels, endeavouring to clear runway, perimeters and dispersals – mainly in the hope of getting a few hours flying in on the morrow'. Despite their best efforts, the wing would not fly a mission again until 13 January. That day, in deplorable conditions, all five squadrons managed to get airborne and fly 98 sorties. The pickings were slim once again, with just two enemy transports damaged.

After six miserable days the wing finally had weather clear enough to send out armed reconnaissance patrols on the 14th. Being in the right place at the right time often spelled success for the young pilots of No 126 Wing, and their luck held that morning. First off at 0935 hrs was No 411 Sqn, followed by Nos 442 and 401 Sqns. At 1020 hrs No 411 Sqn intercepted 11+ Fw 190s over the Cosfeld/Rheine/Hengelo area, and aces Flt Lts R J Audet (in RR201) and J J Boyle (in MK950) claimed a victory apiece, as did Flg Off J A Doran (in PL430). The unit had Flt Lt R J Land (in MH761) killed during this clash, however.

A few minutes later No 401 Sqn 'caught the Hun right in his own backyard' when 12 Fw 190s equipped with 'jet tanks' were bounced in the circuit over Twente airfield – these aircraft were from I./JG 1. Flt Lt

Flg Off J A Doran of No 411 Sqn prepares to start the engine of MK686/DB-L at B88 in March 1945. Doran scored a single victory on 14 January 1945 when he shot down an Fw 190 near Losser, but not in this aircraft. DB-L was the Spitfire that Flt Lt J J Boyle used to spectacularly intercept an Me 262 over the base on Christmas Day 1944 (*Public Archives of Canada 78-337*)

John MacKay (in MJ980) repeated his New Year's day effort by downing three aircraft to 'make ace', while Flt Lt Frederick Murray's single kill (in MJ671) gave him ace status too. Flg Off D B Dack (in NH240) completed the scoring with a solitary victory. No 442 Sqn next entered the fray, having initially provided top cover for No 401 Sqn's initial interception. Flt Lts J E Reade (in PT883) and J N G Dick (in PV154) downed an Fw 190 each, as did Flg Off A J Urquhart (in PL370), although he bailed out into captivity moments later when his fighter was shot up by another Focke-Wulf near Enschede.

FLYING CONTROL

The ability of the young pilots of No 126 Wing to fly in weather that even today would ground the most modern aircraft was a testament to their skill, fortitude and determination. But even those skills could not protect them in every circumstance. Running the air space above the wing's airfield was the responsibility of Flying Control. The area around Nistelrode and Heesch was known for its rapidly changing weather, and that meant thick fog could roll in at a moment's notice. An airfield with marginal flying conditions could go from bad to worse in a just matter of minutes.

It was the job of Flying Control to make sure that pilots could get down before the weather turned bad. Flying Control consisted of a van filled with radios, black boxes and six telephones. From there fighter controllers kept in touch with the pilots above. The Direction Finding Van, known as 'D/F Homer', was also available to aid them in their traffic control duties. The 'Homer's' job was listen to a pilot's frequency and continually take his bearings. When there was an emergency, or a pilot needed a heading home, the D/F operator would inform Flying Control and they would pass that information along to the pilot.

This equipment allowed scores of aircraft and pilots to make their way home through some of the worst weather imaginable. During 11 months of operation 800 homings were passed and 3000 vectors given to 2500 aircraft.

The morning of 20 January dawned with snow squalls, but by 0900 hrs patrols had taken off. The weather held fine until 1240 hrs, when a sudden snow flurry blotted out the base and caused those still in the air to be diverted to Eindhoven. First off was No 411 Sqn on an armed reconnaissance in the Emmerich-Münster-Osnabrück-Lingen area. 'Duff' weather caused the mission to be aborted, but not before Flg Off C A Ellement (in NH380) had been shot down by flak near Nijmegen. On his first operational mission, Ellement evaded capture and made it back to base.

No 412 Sqn was the second unit to depart B88, 11 aircraft taking off at 1020 hrs on an armed reconnaissance to the same area. Only seven Spitfires would return, however. 'Blue section', consisting of Flt Lts B E MacPherson (in PL186) and F H Richards (in ML277) and Plt Offs McPhee (PV352) and W J Walkom (in MJ312) simply vanished. The only sign of trouble was when Flt Lt Richards called to say his engine had cut and he was heading for a field near Nijmegen. It had been a disastrous day for the wing, with five pilots listed not yet returned without explanation.

An Ar 234 is prepared for another mission in early 1945. Not a large aircraft, the Arado bomber shared the same engines and placement as the Me 262. It was not surprising, therefore, when the pilots of No 401 Sqn mistook the aircraft for the more common Me 262, and claimed three shot down and five damaged on 23 January 1945. Flt Lt Audet also downed an Me 262 and destroyed another on the ground that same day (*ww2images.com*)

At the end of the war it was discovered that all four pilots had been captured after making forced landings (most likely due to the weather) in parts of northern Holland with flak-damaged aircraft. Trying to keep under the snow showers by dropping down to 500 ft, they had been picked off by German flak gunners.

Over the next two days the wing mounted 147 sorties, but the results were mixed – one locomotive destroyed, four damaged and four vehicles destroyed.

After some early morning snow the skies turned crisp and clear on the 23rd – a day that was dubbed 'Slaughter of the Me 262s' in the Operational Summary. First off was No 411 Sqn, led by Flt Lt E G Ireland. The unit caught a single Fw 190 in the Lingen-Münster area, which was despatched by Flt Lt R M Cook (in MK950) after he 'caught the lone Hun on the deck' – this was the last of his 3.5 victories.

No 401 Sqn was the next unit to sortie from B88, Sqn Ldr W T Klersy leading his pilots to the Lingen-Osnabrück area. North of the latter town the unit spotted 15 Me 262s taking off and landing at their airfield at Bramsche. The Canadian pilots immediately pounced and came away with an incredible score of three Me 262s destroyed and six more damaged – single kills were credited to Flg Offs D F Church (in ML141) and G A Hardy (in NH240), while Flt Lts W C Connell (in MK791) and M Thomas (in MJ980) shared the third victory.

The next day, after poring over all available recognition manuals, the pilots of No 401 Sqn changed their claims from Me 262s to Ar 234s shot down. It was easy to see how this mistake was made, as they had never seen an Ar 234 before, but after one mission they were now all experts. This encounter graphically illustrated the weakness inherent in German jet technology. While the performance of the Me 262 and Ar 234 was impressive, their engines proved to be their Achilles' heel. Quick throttle movements would cause the powerplants to flame out, and when taking off and landing they were unable to increase their speed quickly and respond to an attack. This is where most of the enemy jets were shot down – while taking off and landing.

No 411 Sqn did encounter Me 262s on its second mission of the day, however. Having headed back to the Lingen-Münster area, 'More joy was in the offing as Flt Lt R J Audet (in RR201) continued to add to his score with two Me 262s destroyed – one on the ground and one in the air'. The unit had Plt Off G G Harrison (in PL433) shot down after he gave chase to two Bf 109s near Osnabrück. He survived this encounter and returned to base on foot.

No 442 Sqn also witnessed the new German jet and rocket technology in the Osnabrück-Münster area, the Operational Summary reporting that 'three Me 262s were seen but could not be engaged.

Spitfire Y2-L of No 442 Sqn has been armed with a single 500-lb bomb on its centreline rack (note the empty wing racks, however) and connected to its battery cart, ready for start up. The aircraft was photographed at Heesch in January 1945. The amount of PSP needed to keep the hard stands and taxiways free of water and mud is clearly evident (*Public Archives of Canada PMR 76-377*)

Three rocket-like flames and trails, possibly from Me 163s, were seen and pinpointed. The things were climbing at about a 90-degree angle, and reached a height of 8000 ft in about 12 seconds'.

For the next three days the weather was 'again duff' and only two sorties were flown. On 24 January No 442 Sqn's Flg Off N A Burns (in PV154) bailed out into captivity after his aircraft was hit by flak near Münster. The 26th saw the arrival of 8.5-victory ace Wg Cdr G W Northcott to replace 'Dal' Russel as the wing's CO.

Conditions cleared sufficiently on the afternoon of 28 January to allow each squadron to perform an armed reconnaissance in the Bremen area. Fifty sorties were flown in total and just three vehicles damaged. The Luftwaffe was also struggling to deal with poor weather conditions, No 411 Sqn pilots reporting that 'snow clearing operations were underway at Twente airfield'. Snowstorms continued to blight western Europe through to the end of the month, allowing only four sorties to be flown.

While January had offered up only a handful of good flying days, No 126 Wing had made the most of them with an impressive 46 aircraft destroyed, three probably destroyed and 17 damaged. Some 1233 sorties had been flown, resulting in a total 1634.18 hours in the air. The price for this aerial success had been a high one, however, with 12 pilots killed or captured. The wing's pilots were rewarded for their efforts with a DSO and nine DFCs.

Having been sat on the ground more often than not for almost a week, the wing managed 46 sorties, and damaged just four vehicles, on 2 February. The Operational Summary for that date opined, 'Although we didn't have a spectacular day, it was good to get aircraft off the ground and discover all the little things that always seem to go wrong when they are not flown regularly'.

The following day would see the wing once again lugging bombs for the first time in 1945, having been reassigned to the rail interdiction programme. Its units flew an impressive 147 sorties and dropped 87 500-lb bombs on various targets. The results, however, were mixed. Three rail cuts were claimed along with eight vehicles, three locomotives and 14 rail cars damaged. The highlight of the day was the destruction of a factory, as described in the Operational Summary;

'The last show led by Flt Lt J J Boyle of No 411 Sqn saw three bombs dropped on a marshalling yard in Rheine. The pilots involved claimed a factory destroyed.'

Yet more poor 'Dutch weather' then rolled in, grounding the wing for two solid days until flying resumed once again on the morning of 6 February. Indeed, the clear conditions would allow the B88-based units to enjoy their busiest day of the month to date. Three squadrons bombed targets while two carried out armed reconnaissance. Amongst the targets attacked was a 'dummy drome' strafed by No 411 Sqn, and the Operational Summary reported that the unit claimed 'a Ju 88 destroyed, and a second Ju 88 and an He 111 damaged – all made of wood (Grr…)'. Totals for the day came to 161 sorties flown and 104 bombs dropped for 16 rail cuts, one locomotive destroyed and five rail cars damaged.

No 442 Sqn was the 'Readiness and Patrol' unit for the day, but the airfield remained 'red' and the pilots were not called on to take-off. 7 February again saw no action, but a message was received from the Senior Operations Officer at No 83 Group highly congratulating No 126 Wing 'on the excellent effort put up yesterday – the best day this year'. Its performance was compared to that of No 143 Wing flying Typhoons, 'whose speciality is bombing, and whose aircraft carry a much heavier load. They scored the same number of rail cuts as 126'.

The wing was off to an early start on 8 February, with the first aircraft from No 402 Sqn being airborne at 0735 hrs. Having suffered terrible serviceability issues with its Spitfire XIVs since joining No 126 Wing in late 1944, the unit claimed its first kill in 1945 when Flt Lt K S Sleep (in RM862) downed a lone Ju 88 nightfighter from NJG 2 that was on an air test north of Coesfeld.

No 442 Sqn had taken off shortly after No 402 Sqn, and at 0840 hrs the unit 'hit the jackpot' when it spotted five Ju 87s southeast of Wesel. By this late stage of the war it was very unusual to see the antiquated Junkers dive-bomber in the air during daylight, and the pilots of No 442 Sqn made short work of the formation. All five were shot down, with two and one shared being claimed by Flt Lt D C Gordon (in PV148), one and one shared credited to Flt Lt J G Doyle (in MJ464) and a single kill to Flt Lt R B Barker (in MK898). This was the first of four victories and two damaged that Barker would claim.

The bohemian way of squadron life within the 2nd TAF called for inventive thinking. Here, three groundcrewmen from No 442 Sqn stand in front of their 'Waco' trailer. Fitted with surplus Spitfire wheels, the salvaged front fuselage of an American Waco glider was equipped for life on the road. It is not clear if the glider was modified in Normandy or Holland (*Public Archives of Canada PMR 76-371*)

As the weather closed in No 411 Sqn flew two 'Rhubarbs' that afternoon with unfortunate, but familiar, results. German flak remained the greatest danger to the pilots of No 126 Wing, and Flt Lt R J Audet (in PL430) would experience this at first hand at 1515 hrs. The Operational Summary recorded;

'Flt Lt R J Audet and Flg Off R C McCracken went on the first "Rhubarb" to Twente Aerodrome. They made the trip over the deck.

No 411 Sqn's Flt Lt Dick Audet, who was No 126 Wing's 'ace in a day', or more accurately 'ace in a single sortie'. Not only did Audet shoot down five enemy fighters, he did it in a matter of minutes, and remarkably they were his first aerial victories of the war. He would go on to score five more victories, bringing his score to 10.5 (including one Me 262 shot down and one damaged). He was awarded the DFC in February and a Bar in March 1945, the latter being announced shortly after Audet was killed on 3 March while strafing a train (*DND PL 41192*)

When they reached the 'drome they found only a handful of workmen about. A well-camouflaged gun position opened up on them. Flg Off McCracken returned the fire with all he had, and although no claims are submitted, he must have made it quite warm for them. Flt Lt Audet received some flak from the northern end of the 'drome and his aircraft was hit, and badly damaged, by the first few bursts. He thought he would have to bail out, but by careful nursing he was able to bring the aircraft back to base. He could not land, however, as the aircraft refused to remain straight and level when he cut the speed. Audet ended up climbing to a safe altitude and bailing out well in sight of all ground personnel, who saw both the aircraft and Dick come down. He was very lucky to hit a soft field, being picked up immediately by a chap on a motorcycle, transferred to a jeep and driven back to Intelligence in time for interrogation.'

GROUNDCREW

No 126 Wing's success had as much to do with the skill and courage of its pilots as it did with the skill and professionalism of its groundcrew. Without the latter, the pilots would have had no aircraft to fly. Having a reliable machine meant that missions were flown with few returns, and squadrons could fly their full complement of aircraft on a continuous basis. For the month of January the wing's Chief Technical Officer released figures for overall serviceability of aircraft by squadron. Top of the list was No 401 Sqn with 88.3 percent, and the overall wing figure was a highly commendable 84.4 percent.

Clear patches of weather greeted the wing at dawn on 11 February, although by mid-morning conditions had completely closed in, forcing patrols to be recalled. While just 53 sorties were flown during the course of the day, No 402 Sqn had Flt Lt W G Hodges (in RN118) killed when he crashed northeast of Volkel after losing his formation while descending through cloud to land. At 1400 hrs Flg Off A T Gibbs (in PT535) took to his parachute when his fighter suffered an engine failure near Cleve. Gibb hitchhiked back to base.

More bad weather meant that just 19 sorties were flown on 12/13 February, although on the former date No 402 Sqn's Flg Off W D Wittaker (in RM846) limped back to base with a badly damaged machine after hitting high-tension power cables while strafing a train. The Spitfire was declared unrepairable and scrapped.

The loss of two Spitfires and a pilot in 48 hours was just the latest setback to befall No 402 Sqn. There had been much grumbling from within the unit since the new year about the fact that it was still waiting for the 'last few bits and pieces necessary to make the Spitfire XIV

a fighter-bomber'. Indeed, at wing level there was some concern that the squadron was not inflicting as much damage on the enemy as it could. This resulted in ever more rancorous protests from within No 402 Sqn. Despite all the 'belly aching', the unit still had to wait until 22 February to receive external shackles that finally allowed bombs to be carried on the Spitfire XIV.

Strong crosswinds were the order of the day when No 126 Wing took to the air on 14 February and recorded 237 sorties – 'the largest number since its arrival on the Continent' according to the Operational Summary. A number of 'jet jobs' were reported as 'elusive in the air all day', and No 411 Sqn spotted '30+ glistening twin-engined aircraft lined up in full view at Münster-Handorf aerodrome'. These were He 177 bombers, and Flt Lt J J Boyle (in PV230) claimed two destroyed and one damaged and Flt Sgt J O A Watt (in PV347) two more damaged during a strafing pass. No 401 Sqn also spotted a gaggle of 10+ Ar 234s and two Me 262s but they could not be caught. Nevertheless, the Canadian pilots succeeded in dispersing the enemy formation.

Dive-bombing and rail cuts were also the order of the day, and the dropping of 152 bombs resulted in 14 cuts being made, three locomotives and six rail cars destroyed and 28 damaged.

Between 16 and 20 February weather once again limited the wing to just 98 sorties, all of which were flown on the 16th.

The morning of the 21st was initially blighted by ground haze, but the weather cleared over the target area to permit a full afternoon of flying to take place. All five squadrons conducted missions in the Emmerich, Lingen, Vesel, Münster, Dorsten, Borken and Boochalt areas, the results of which were nine cuts, three locomotives destroyed and eight damaged, along with 33 rail cars and eight vehicles damaged. But these successes cost No 402 Sqn two Spitfires and one pilot. Flt Lt L G 'Lem' Barnes' fighter (RM839) was hit by flak and he bailed out over enemy-held territory near Haltern, although the pilot evaded. The fighter flown by Barnes' wingman, Flg Off J C McAllister (in RM758),

No 412 Sqn Spitfires undergo maintenance at Heesch in March 1945. Serviceability rates for No 126 Wing were excellent, with numbers in the mid to high 80 percentile. This was a remarkable achievement considering most if not all maintenance had to be done out doors, no matter what the weather (*DND PL 42422*)

also suffered flak damage, but the young Canadian succeeded in coaxing it back to B88. However, he crashed heavily attempting to land and subsequently died of the injuries he had suffered in the accident.

The following day a further 192 sorties were flown, achieving 'fair results'. But three more Spitfires were also destroyed and a pilot killed. No 412 Sqn had flown the first mission of the day, and during the return flight to base Flt Lt Bill Cowan (in PL252) suffered engine failure and bailed out six miles east of Heesch. The pilot struck the tailplane of the aircraft as he jumped, knocking him unconscious and preventing him from deploying his parachute. Upon landing, No 412 Sqn's CO, Sqn Ldr M D Boyd, quickly proceeded by road to the area where Cowan had abandoned his fighter and duly discovered the pilot's lifeless body. Losses such as this one were keenly felt by the whole wing, and it was even harder to take now that the end of the war in Europe was well within sight. A grim resolve began to characterise operations as the weather, accidents and enemy action continued to take more lives.

During No 401 Sqn's second show of the day heavy flak north of Hengelo brought down the Spitfire (MJ851) of ace Flt Lt Freddie Murray. He crash-landed in enemy territory and was soon captured. A few minutes later No 442 Sqn lost its CO, and ace, Sqn Ldr M E Jowsey (in PT725), when his fighter was hit by his own bullets ricocheting off vehicles that he was in the process of strafing near Emmerich! He bailed out and was observed to land by other members of his units, who reported that he was 'okay'. Jowsey successfully evaded capture, although he never returned to No 442 Sqn – his place was taken by Sqn Ldr M Johnson.

This unit suffered two more casualties at 1010 hrs on 24 February when Bf 109s were spotted at low-level in the Rhine river area. Formation leaders Flg Offs J G Doyle (in MJ464) and J A T E Cousineau (in NH489), and their wingmen, set off in pursuit of them, and the latter pilot was credited with a Messerschmitt destroyed. Neither pilot returned to B88, however, both having been shot down and killed by either German fighters or flak – Boyle was seen to bail out, but he did not survive.

No 442 Sqn reaped its revenge the following day, although the weather did its best to prevent the unit from finding the enemy. The morning began with a 'full flying programme', but it would not last. The Operational Summary noted, 'Weather conditions in Hun land were not quite so favourable, and soon after all suitable areas were too heavily overcast to allow any pickings. As well, the annoying crosswind at base had accelerated to the point of being downright embarrassing to many pilots'. Nevertheless, 'Three squadrons tested the fruit of aerial combat as outlined below, with the day's laurels going to No 442 Sqn

Having completed yet another sortie, Sqn Ldr M D Boyd is helped out of his parachute at Heesch in the spring of 1945. He had assumed command of No 412 Sqn on 14 January 1945, having previously served with this unit as a flight commander in 1942-43. Boyd rejoined the unit in October 1944, and he claimed four and one shared destroyed and one damaged between 24 December 1944 and 30 April 1945 (*Public Archives of Canada PMR 78-303*)

with seven Me 109s destroyed and one damaged for no loss. No 412 Sqn's first foursome on Enschede patrols turned a Hun bounce into one Me 109 destroyed and one damaged, while No 402 Sqn's sextet on its way home from a bombing show got tired of letting Me 262s whistle by unmolested, so they chase one and knocked some pieces off it'.

The first kill was claimed by No 412 Sqn's Flg Off H W McLeod (in RK900) at 0800 hrs when one of its four-aircraft patrols encountered two groups of Bf 109s (each eight-strong in number) near Enschede. At 0835 hrs Plt Off R V Watson (in PK992) was hit by flak while dive-bombing near Wesel and he was forced to bail out. He successfully made it back to B88. Ten minutes later Flt Lts K S Sleep (in RM862) and B E Innes (in RM726) from No 402 Sqn damaged an Me 262 near Twente. The unit had Flt Lt W S Harvey (in RM906) shot down by flak near Enschede at 0905 hrs, and although he was initially captured, he escaped six weeks later.

The last kills of the day were claimed by pilots from No 442 Sqn, who took off on a sweep of the Lingen-Wesel area at 1053 hrs. They intercepted 40+ Bf 109s from II. and IV./JG 27 west of Rheine. Ace Flt Lt D C Gordon (in PV148) claimed one, while Flt Lts R K Trumley (in PL423) and R B Barker (in MK844) and Plt Off E C Baker (in PT883) got two each.

The day's results were good, with eight enemy fighters shot down and three damaged. The wing had also dropped 91 bombs for nine rail cuts, one locomotive and three rail cars destroyed and one flak tower damaged.

The Spitfire's ability to absorb a great deal of damage (as long as its engine was not too badly hit) and yet still bring its pilot home was graphically shown once again during the action of 25 February. Flt Lt Reid of No 411 Sqn returned to base with three feet of one propeller blade shorn off. He made 'a superb emergency landing' that was a credit to his piloting skill in what was described as the 'worst-shaped aircraft ever flown in'. The engine had sprung several oil leaks, the oil tank was hanging by one clamp after it had vibrated off its moorings, the air intake scoop was all but shot away, the engine bearers were bent, the front engine-bearer bolts were sheared, the fuselage was distorted and the vibration in the cockpit had been so bad that it had knocked the pilot's helmet off!

February ended better than it had began, with 153 sorties flown on the 28th. Wg Cdr Geoff Northcott's Operational Summary for the month makes for interesting reading, and portions of it are quoted below;

'February was not quite as bad a month for weather as it might have been, with exactly half of the 28 days being flyable more or less. Although the good days were no more than in January, a substantial increase in sorties was achieved by each squadron. The wing total for five squadrons was 1698 sorties, with 1997 ops hours flown, compared to 1233 sorties with 1643 hours the previous month. On 14 February the Wing set an all-time record for itself with 237 sorties, representing a turnaround of four shows per aircraft.

'The versatility of the Spitfire as a fighter-bomber was re-established as the wing built up fair scores in air-to-air combat, ground strafing and dive-bombing. Bombing, with three squadrons active on it most of the month, was resumed after a total lapse of a month, and while less than half the total weight was dropped, the 98 rail cuts came within three of our previous high month of November 1944.

'During armed reconnaissance, enemy road and rail transport was found on a larger, though not lavish, scale – nine enemy vehicles were destroyed and 146 damaged, which was more than triple the January score. Locomotives were also found moving more often than the previous month, with No 402 Sqn claiming the Lion's share of the 13 destroyed and 40 damaged bag. Goods trucks (both open and closed, and often laden), while still being claimed conservatively, totalled 250 destroyed and damaged.

'In the air, the score of 16 enemy aircraft destroyed and seven damaged was modest in comparison with the 46 destroyed, four probables and 15 damaged of the previous month, but 1 January activity represents most of the difference.

'In respect to enemy tactics, as the month rolled on another trend became evident. Hun aircraft were engaged successfully four times in the second half of the month, compared to only twice for the first half. And they were reported, but not seen, more often still. The Hun apparently had been given a "shot-in-the-arm" and showed a decided inclination to stay and fight more frequently. The once-familiar tactic of "sucker bait", with a few Huns apparently by themselves, was witnessed on several occasions, but the resulting engagements showed that bounces by the Hun still turned in our favour.

'Nothing in the month's activities indicated the desirability to make basic changes in current tactics. However, steady modifications have been made in the light of changing conditions and increased experience. It is considered that dive-bombing efforts are best undertaken in flight strength, with the flights alternating as top cover. Nearly all air-to-air engagements demonstrated the close adherence of the enemy to the practice of stepped up formations, and continued to prove the absolute necessity of a careful watch for a bounce from above prior to, and during, the engagement of any enemy formation.

'Losses in the wing were once again high, with ten pilots missing or killed, compared to 12 the previous month. No generalised reason for the losses can readily be found, other than straight bad luck. Flak was a constant worry, but is not known to have accounted for more than two, or possibly three. Enemy air efforts may have caused two more. The balance were lost either in accidents or incidents not known to be due to enemy action. Losses of formation leaders were disproportionately high, with one squadron commander and three flight commanders recorded as not yet returned.

'Accidents due to other than technical failures totalled four for the month, three being Category AC (repairable) and one Category E (written off). This represented one flying accident for every 449 flying hours. However, January was the perfect month, with no accidents known to have been due to other than technical failures.

'The conversion of aircraft to 150 octane fuel towards the end of the month was accomplished with no grief or untoward incidents thus far. Wing serviceability maintained a high average, with 86.4 percent compared to 84.4 percent in January.'

A No 126 Wing Spitfire is fuelled up at Heesch during the long winter of 1945. This Spitfire is equipped with a 30-gallon slipper tank and wing racks for two 250-lb bombs. This photograph clearly illustrates the limitations of the Spitfire as a fighter-bomber. When it did carry its full complement of 1000 lbs of bombs, it could not fly very far, and when more fuel was added bomb load had to be sacrificed (*Public Archives of Canada PL 41494*)

March began with Nos 401 and 412 Sqns being 'bounced by 40+ Me 109s and Fw 190s in the Dorsten area' at 0910 hrs. No 412 Sqn was unable to get involved, but No 401 Sqn 'mixed it up' with JGs 26 and 27 and achieved impressive results. Sqn Ldr W T Klersy (in MH847) shot down 'two Me 109s' and then destroyed an Fw 190 from a formation that was spotted after the unit had reformed following the first clash. Fellow high-scoring ace Flt Lt John MacKay (in MJ854) also destroyed an Fw 190 and damaged another, as well as a Bf 109.

No 401 Sqn did not emerge from the engagement unscathed, however, as Flt Lt H P M Furniss (in EN569) was shot down by a Bf 109. Nothing more was seen or heard of him, Furniss spending the last few weeks of the war as a PoW. Flt Lt O E Thorpe (in MJ448) had his aileron controls shot away in the same action, and with both hands on the control column he managed to limp home and perform a 195 mph wheels-up landing at Volkel!

The day's haul brought No 126 Wing's total score since formation to 302 enemy aircraft destroyed, 273 of them since D-Day.

In an effort to surprise the Germans, No 401 Sqn took off just prior to dawn on 2 March. The unit met with no success, however, and by 0715 hrs all five squadron were airborne. Again, all sweeps were uneventful. A few trains were spotted, but the wing's ability to attack them had now been stopped through the issuing of the 'No Ground Attack' rule by 2nd TAF HQ. A quote from the Operational Summary reveals how unpopular this decision was;

'The new system of flying was rather hard to take as we stood by for the balance of the morning and part of the afternoon before new jobs were given to us and flying was resumed.'

On 3 March, while the other squadrons 'saw a lot of stuff on the ground but were not allowed to attack it', Flt Lt R J Audet's No 411 Sqn either disobeyed the order or had not received it as they shot up a train near Coesfeld with depressing results. During the attack Flt Lt Audet – who had just returned from a week's leave – was hit by flak. His aircraft (MK950) started pouring glycol and quickly burst into

Spitfires of No 401 Sqn taxi out at Heesch in March 1945. ML141/YO-E was being piloted by Flg Off D F Church when it shot down an Ar 234 over Bramsche airfield on 24 January 1945. Church would end the war with two Bf 109s and one Ar 234 destroyed and one Bf 109 damaged to his credit (*Public Archives of Canada PA 115093*)

flames, diving into a wood from a height of 500 ft and exploding. Audet was killed instantly. His death was a tremendous loss for the RCAF, for at just 22 years of age he had amassed an impressive score of 10.5 kills and one damaged in 83 sorties.

No 126 Wing would not encounter the Luftwaffe again in the air until 12 March, having spent the intervening time flying sweeps and patrols without any real success to speak of. Finally, during the very last sweep of the day on the 12th, No 401 Sqn's Flt Lt L N Watt (in MK203) 'spotted an Me 262 zooming along below cloud at 2500 ft in the area just west of Wesel. Flt Lt Watt gave him a short burst, saw him go down in smoke but had to break off due to very accurate fire from our own guns. The Me 262 was later confirmed by the Army as destroyed'.

The following day another jet (identified by the pilot as an Me 262, but deemed to be an Ar 234 by 2nd TAF HQ after gun camera film was examined) was shot down by Flg Off Howard Nicholson (RM875) of No 402 Sqn while flying a late afternoon sweep near Gladback. His combat report read as follows;

'I was flying "Yellow 3" on a fighter sweep in the Gladback area when I sighted a ME 262 at about 5000 ft flying southwest. He did not appear to see me. I broke and fired a three-second burst from 250 yards line astern into his starboard wing and the base of the fuselage. Smoke poured out and pieces flew off the starboard wing. I kept firing, observing many hits, and the aircraft tended to fall out of control, regaining slowly. At 2000 ft he went into a sharp dive to port, but owing to the extremely heavy flak from Gladback, I broke to starboard. I did not see him crash, but this is confirmed by the CO of No 402 Sqn. I claim one ME 262 destroyed. '

Me 262s were also active when No 442 Sqn completed a sweep at around the same time, the unit's pilots sighting six of them. These were duly attacked, but the Spitfires were unable to close to an effective range. Another jet was spotted south of Goch, but the RCAF pilots were again unable to press home an attack due to the very intense anti-aircraft fire that was presumably being aimed at the Me 262.

The only other event of note on 13 March resulted in the loss of No 401 Sqn Spitfire MK888, flown by Flg Off A R W McKay. The fighter suffered engine trouble near Borken and the pilot bailed out.

After several days freed from dive-bombing and ground attacks, No 126 Wing returned to its rail interdiction programme on the 15th, scoring 15 cuts and destroying a petrol dump during the course of 115

sorties. Two days later the wing again got the chance to add to its tally of aerial victories when No 412 Sqn claimed two Fw 190Ds (from III./JG 26) following a late afternoon dive-bombing mission. Sqn Ldr M D Boyd (in PV234) and Flg Off V Smith (in PV253) shared one between them, while Plt Off H W Grant (in PV202) got the other fighter.

No 412 Sqn, and the remaining four units in the wing, had been assigned a special target that day – 'a German Stragglers' Post in a little village east of Wesel'. All squadrons sent 12 aircraft against it, and each unit was led by their respective COs. It was a good day, with 15 tons of bombs dropped on Germany, three direct hits on the briefed target, two Fw 190s shot down and five rail cuts. This proved to be the last mission flown by No 442 Sqn with No 126 Wing, for on 22 March it was sent back to the UK to re-equip with Mustang IIIs and rejoin Fighter Command. The following month the unit started flying bomber escort missions from RAF Digby, in Lincolnshire.

Forward airfields were a Godsend for other Allied aircraft and crews. Often damaged, or with wounded men on board, they would land at the nearest friendly airfield. Here, a Spitfire from No 412 Sqn taxis past B-26G-1 *LA PALOMA* of the 553rd BS/386th BG at Heesch on 22 March 1945 (*Public Archives of Canada PA 115100*)

Four No 412 Sqn Spitfires line up on either side of the runway on 22 March 1945. Both pairs are angled towards the centreline of the runway, ready for departure. It was an uneventful day for the wing, with just a No 412 Sqn Spitfire suffering an engine failure on take-off (*Public Archives of Canada PA 115091*)

MK193/Y2-E of No 442 Sqn taxis by the camera also on 22 March 1945. The bomb racks have disappeared but small 30-gallon slipper tanks are evident. By March the wing no longer carried out any dive-bombing missions, concentrating instead on armed reconnaissance and fighter sweeps (*Public Archives of Canada PA 115092*)

CROSSING THE RHEINE

Spring would see the Allied armies on the west bank of the Rhine poised for the final great battle of the war in western Europe. Montgomery's 21st Army Group, which included the British Second Army and the US Ninth Army, would lead the way, with the assault – codenamed Operation *Plunder* – set for the evening of 23 March. That afternoon Typhoons from No 121 Wing and the Spitfires of No 126 Wing were tasked with anti-flak missions. Their job was to attack German flak positions that were beyond the range of Allied artillery.

Plunder began with a tremendous barrage from 1300 British, Canadian and American guns. Under the cover of a smoke screen, amphibious forces began their crossing of the Rhine – Germany's last natural defensive barrier.

The following day Operation *Varsity* was launched – 'the most successful and well executed airborne operation of the war'. Two airborne divisions were involved (the British 6th and the US 17th) and they were transported to their drop zones in a massive armada of 4000 aircraft and gliders, escorted by 1200 fighters. After landing in their assigned zones the airborne forces were charged with seizing and holding the bridges across the River Ijssel until relieved by ground forces at 1800 hrs.

No 126 Wing played its part by providing standing patrols at 12,000 ft between the cities of Zutphen and Winteswijk. Although the skies were filled with Allied aircraft, the Luftwaffe failed to show. Flak would take the heaviest toll, despite the anti-flak operations flown immediately prior to the battle. A total of 219 sorties were generated by the wing, with the only claims being made by No 402 Sqn, whose pilots shot up a number of ground targets. It had been a busy day nevertheless, with No 411 Sqn being the first up shortly after dawn and No 412 Sqn the last to land at 1835 hrs. The day's only casualty was Flt Lt A A W Orr (in NH438) of No 411 Sqn, who was injured when his fighter suffered an engine failure on take-off and crashed at B88.

Spitfire RN119/AE-J was regularly flown by Sqn Ldr Leslie Moore of No 402 Sqn in the early months of 1945. Unfortunately, Moore fell victim to enemy flak or ricochets while attacking a train in the Hamm-Münster area on 25 March 1945, his aircraft (MV258) diving straight into the ground. Moore's final score was three and three shared destroyed, one probable and one and one shared damaged – these successes had come with No 402 Sqn in 1943 and No 441 Sqn in 1944. Flg Off Brian McConnell subsequently shot down an Ar 234 with RN119 on 19 April 1945 (*Public Archives of Canada PL 42423*)

War is always arbitrary. No matter your rank or experience, death was always lurking on the edges waiting to strike. US citizen Sqn Ldr Leslie Moore was given command of No 402 Sqn on 22 February 1945 and one month later he was killed in action (*No 402 Sqn Archives*)

No 412 Sqn Spitfires have their engines run up prior to departing Heesch in the spring of 1945. Remarkably, the vast majority of fighters in the 2nd TAF were Spitfire IXs, despite this variant having first entered service in June 1942. Indeed, R J Mitchell's ingenious design still had the performance to take on the best piston-engined fighters the Luftwaffe had to offer, including the superb Fw 190D and new Bf 109K (*Public Archives of Canada PA 116491*)

25 March proved to be just as busy, but far more productive in terms of aerial victories. The day got off to a bad start, however, when No 402 Sqn's CO, and ace, Sqn Ldr L A Moore (in MV258), was shot down and killed while attacking a train in the Hamn-Münster area at 0730 hrs. His fighter was either hit by German flak or ricochets from his own guns.

At 1810 hrs, No 412 Sqn bounced 15 Fw 190Ds of II. and IV./JG 26 over Bocholt while patrolling between Zutphen and Winterswijk. The Canadian pilots, who misidentified the long-nosed Focke-Wulfs as Bf 109s, claimed three victories, with Sqn Ldr M D Boyd (in PV202), Flt Lt D M Pieri (in NH471) and Flg Off V Smith (in PV253) each claiming a fighter apiece.

The wing experienced two more losses to flak the following day. The first to go down was No 411 Sqn's Flg Off R C McCracken (in MJ463), who was hit while attacking a train west of Hamm at 0708 hrs. He bailed out and evaded back to Allied lines. At 1310 hrs Flt Lt J G Burchill (in MJ650) of No 412 Sqn took to his parachute after his fighter was targeted northwest of Dorsten. He too evaded.

The last few days of March would see the Allied armies continue to push into Germany. No 126 Wing did not lose a beat, with more ground attack missions and air-to-air victories. On the 28th Flt Lt John MacKay (in MJ854) of No 401 Sqn encountered six Bf 109s and shot one down near Dulmen-Coesfeld and the other over Münster. These victories took his tally to nine and two shared. Two days later Flt Lt H A Cowan (in RM727) of No 402 Sqn caught 16 Fw 190Ds of I. and IV./JG 26 during a late afternoon strafing mission southwest of Oldenburg and managed to shoot one of them down. Earlier that same day No 412 Sqn had had Flt Lt W J Anderson (in MJ275) killed when his fighter was hit by flak in the drop tank and crashed in flames near

No 402 Sqn pilots come together for a group shot in early March 1945. Sqn Ldr L A Moore can be seen third from right in the front row (*No 402 Sqn Archive*)

Zelhem during an armed reconnaissance. Squadronmate Flt Lt W R James (in PT357) was also hit at the same time, but he bailed out near Rees and was captured.

On the 31st No 402 Sqn again tasted success when aircraft on the first of four armed reconnaissance missions flown by the unit that day encountered Fw 190Ds of 5./JG 26 south of Oldenburg. Flg Off R W Lawson (in RM804) claimed two destroyed and Flt Lt B E Innes (in MV302) one.

As the Allied forces pushed deeper into Germany, several No 126 Wing pilots previously listed as missing began to turn up. Flt Lt Bill Harvey of No 402 Sqn, who had bailed out over Germany in February, returned after escaping from his PoW camp. Flg Off Harry Furniss of No 401 Sqn was also welcomed back after being found by American troops. Next to come home was Flg Off C A E Ellement of No 411 Sqn, and on 3 April No 442 Sqn ace Flt Lt Milt Jowsey returned. It was a welcome change of pace, and of the 79 pilots listed as missing since D-Day, 21 had now returned to the wing.

Continuing its run of recent form, No 402 Sqn claimed the wing's first aerial victories of the month when, on the 5th, six aircraft intercepted five Fw 190Ds from IV./JG 26 in the Lingen-Rheine area. The Canadians claimed to have run into 20 Fw 190s and Bf 109s! Flg Off A G Ratcliffe (in RM119) was credited with one Bf 109 shot down and Flt Lt W F Peck (in RM843) came away with an Fw 190 destroyed. The squadron also damaged two Fw 190s and two Bf 109s.

BASE MOVE

After its long stay at B88, No 126 Wing was finally on the move. An advance party left on 8 April for B100 Goch, in Germany, and two days later it continued on to B108 Rheine. But the upheaval was not yet over, for on the 13th Grp Capt McGregor had flown ahead to discover that B116 Wunstorf was available. Firm arrangements were quickly made and the wing's first convoys set out that same day bound for their new base at B116.

The trip to Wunstorf was a challenge for the men involved in moving the wing's necessities. Accidents were not uncommon as traffic clogged the roads and refugees and PoWs pushed back in the opposite direction. In the following days some sections were lost for brief periods after taking wrong turns along the unmarked roads. Eventually everyone arrived.

The hard work and frustration was amply rewarded, for B116 was a permanent Luftwaffe base that

had been largely left intact. The speed of the Allied advance had given the Germans little time to evacuate and no demolition had taken place. There were also a number of abandoned, but still intact, Luftwaffe aircraft on thr airfield, including a Dornier Do 335 Pfeil. This late development fighter was equipped with two engines – one in the front and one in the back in a push-pull arrangement. The aircraft was of great interest to Allied Intelligence, but it was destroyed when a fuel bowser parked nearby caught fire.

While Wunstorf was soon proving popular with both air- and groundcrew – it boasted a cinema, gymnasium, outdoor pool and playing field – the war continued around them. On 10 April, just prior to the base move, Flg Off V Smith (in MK844) suffered an engine fire whilst on a patrol and bailed out over Almelo. He was quickly reunited with No 412 Sqn. Sadly, No 402 Sqn's Flg Off G F Peterson (in RM904) was not so fortunate, as he was killed when his fighter was downed by flak near Arnhem on the 11th.

On 14 April No 402 Sqn lost its newly minted CO of just eight days, and ranking 2nd TAF ace of 1944-45, Sqn Ldr Don Laubman. Right at the beginning of his second tour, Laubman (in NH744) attacked a pair of German halftracks in the Rethem area. After shooting up the first vehicle, he lined up the second one just as his previous target exploded. The subsequent fireball engulfed his brand new Spitfire XIV, literally cooking its Griffon engine. Climbing to 7000 ft with his engine temperature rapidly rising, Laubman headed for Allied territory. Unfortunately his damaged Spitfire burst into flames and he was forced to bail out into captivity. Laubman subsequently rejoined his unit on 5 May.

Throughout the transition from B108 to B116 the wing continued to fly armed reconnaissance missions. Indeed, on 15 April Nos 401, 402, 411 and 412 Sqns began their day flying out of B108 in search of ground targets, after which most pilots recovered at B116. No 401 Sqn's WO Campbell (in PL278) actually force-landed at the new base at 1355 hrs after suffering flak damage – his fighter was declared a write-off. And while the wing was still flying its missions, the supply situation became critical due to its rapid move to the northeast. By 16 April the servicing echelons were stretched to the limit, with both petrol and ammunition being unavailable. An emergency airlift

Although of indifferent quality, this photograph is important nevertheless as it shows Spitfires from No 411 Sqn taxiing in at B116 Wunstorf for the very first time on 14 April 1945. This airfield would be No 126 Wing's last operational base in World War 2. Remarkably, Wunstorf was found to be totally intact by No 126 Wing, the base boasting both a functioning cinema and outdoor pool (*Public Archives of Canada PMR 78-54*)

Flt Lt D J Dewan and Flg Off V Smith of No 412 Sqn at B88 Heesch in March 1945. Smith, who would finish the war with 2.5 aerial victories to his name, was forced to bail out of Spitfire MK844 after it suffered an engine fire on 10 April 1945 (*Public Archives of Canada PMR 78-301*)

April would see Allied forces moving rapidly into Germany. Keeping pace was vital, and in some cases it meant spending only days at an airfield before moving on. Here, two No 412 Sqn Spitfire IXs line up for take-off at B108 Rheine. No 126 Wing would occupy this base for just three days from 13 to 16 April 1945 (*Public Archives of Canada PA 136915*)

VZ-N of No 412 Sqn kicks up a cloud of dust as it accelerates down the PSP runway at B108 Rheine in April, 1945. Since D-Day, the tempo of operations had been very high, and the wear and tear on men and machines was constant. Indeed, No 126 Wing had gone through 325 Spitfires since 6 June 1944, 153 of which were returned to service, 102 were completely written off and 70 were missing (*Public Archives of Canada PA 136916*)

was organised which produced 20,000 rounds of 20 mm ammunition and some essential lubricants, but fuel remained a problem.

While the supply situation caused headaches for some Allied units, it was beyond catastrophic for the Germans. As of 12 April the 2nd TAF faced a mere 63 serviceable Fw 190s of JG 26 and 55 serviceable Bf 109s of JG 27, plus a handful of airworthy Me 262s and Ar 234 jet bombers.

On the morning of the 17th an emergency convoy left B116 for an armament park in order to redress the situation. Ground attack operations consumed vast quantities of bombs and ammunition, and following the success of Operations *Plunder* and *Varsity* in late March, No 126 Wing had continued with its road and rail interdiction missions. Pilots found plenty of ground targets as the Germans continued to retreat, and the sortie tempo was intense as squadrons refuelled and rearmed and took off once again in search of anything that moved. They also managed to add to their score of aerial and strafing victories too.

At 0745 hrs on 16 April Flt Lt J MacKay (in MJ854) of No 401 Sqn made a solo attack on Ludwigslust airfield that resulted in three Ar 234s being damaged before the plucky Canadian was forced to break off his attack due to heavy flak. The latter knocked down squadronmate Flt L W Woods (in MJ390) near Wunstorf on the same patrol, however, although he successfully evaded. No 402 Sqn's Flt Lt J E Maurice (in RM843) failed to return from a mid-morning patrol over Salzwedel, although he rejoined the unit on 5 May. At 1400 hrs Flg Off C D W Wilson (in RR201) of No 411 Sqn could not believe his luck when he spotted a lone He 111 near Grabow. He quickly shot it down for the first of his five kills, three of which would come in 1948 while flying Spitfire IXs for the Israeli Defence Force against the Royal Egyptian Air Force.

This day would also see the destruction of the first 'Mistel' composite aircraft by the wing when Flt Lt D C Gordon (in NH251) and Flg Off D J Bazett (in MK686) found this most unusual, and tempting, target while searching for vehicles to strafe. Spotted at low-level headed for the bridges at Kurstrin, this hybrid consisted of an Fw 190 attached to the top of an explosive laden, and pilotless, Ju 88. Once in the target area the Fw 190 would detach from the Ju 88 and the pilot would guide the bomber to the objective. It was a cumbersome operation, and an easy target.

Flt Lt Gordon opened fire at 500 yards and the Fw 190 quickly detached from the Ju 88, which burst into flames and crashed in a huge fireball. Flg Off Bazett stayed with the Fw 190 and shot it down in short order. Both men were credited with a shared victory over a single composite aircraft by 2nd TAF.

Things got off to a bad start on 17 April when Flg Off L A Dunn (in ML342) was killed at 0725 hrs while attacking a train between Lubeck and Kyritz. Unbeknownst to him, the wagons he strafed were carrying barrels of fuel, causing the train to explode just as he flew over it. Dunn had just returned to No 401 Sqn for his second tour. At 1100 hrs, during No 401 Sqn's second patrol of the day, Flg Off J P W Francis (in MH479) shot down a 'Bf 109' – actually an Fw 190D – from I./JG 26 overhead Ludwigslust airfield. At the end of that mission, Sqn Ldr W T Klersy (in MH847) force-landed at B116 in a flak-damaged Spitfire that subsequently burnt itself out on the grass runway.

Ammunition shortages continued to plague the wing, despite the arrival of another 20,000 rounds by air, and petrol also remained in short supply. Urgent requests were sent and the result was the promise of 13 Dakotas! The plan was for these aircraft to deliver two shipments in one day, but in the end only nine aircraft made one delivery. Priority orders had the Dakotas assigned to casualty evacuation, leaving the wing to struggle on as best it could.

The grass airfield at B116 was also beginning to disintegrate under the strain of both transport aircraft and fighters. The forward location of Wunstorf made it the prime destination for dignitaries and other people of importance visiting the frontline, and this resulted in a number of missions being cancelled on the 18th due to the almost non-stop arrival of transport aircraft. Two of the fighters that did manage to take off on that date failed to return to base. Flt Lt D R Drummond (in RN126) of No 402 Sqn force-landed near B116 after his aircraft was hit by flak and No 412 Sqn's Flt Lt R B Barker (in MK898) ran out of fuel and crash-landed in no man's land between Lübeck and Goldberg. He returned to base on foot.

The situation at B116 greatly improved on the 19th when the new metal landing strip was completed and reserved almost exclusively for the wing's Spitfires – the old grass strip was used by transport aircraft only. A full day's 'ops' followed, which resulted in an impressive score. A mid-morning armed reconnaissance by No 412 Sqn saw the unit

In this view of No 401 Sqn's RN119 at Heesch in March 1945, it can be seen that the aircraft still retains the old Mk II gunsight, rather than the more effective GM2 (*No 402 Sqn Archives*)

engage at least six Fw 190s over Hagenow airfield, four of which were shot down. Flt Lt D M Pieri (in NH471) 'made ace' when he claimed one and one shared with Flt Lt L A Stewart (in MJ504). Single victories were also credited to Flt Lt D J Dewan (in MJ795) and Flg Off G M Horter (in PL448). A short time later No 402 Sqn also intercepted a gaggle of Fw 190s in the same area and Flg Off H C Dutton (in RM902) claimed one more destroyed – a further three were damaged.

No 402 Sqn was back in the air on its second armed reconnaissance of the day in the early afternoon, and at 1410 hrs Flg Off C B MacConnell (in RN119) caught a Ju 88 north of the Schweriner See and shot it down. Flt Lt H A Cowan (in RN204) was shot down and killed by flak over Parchim airfield during the same mission.

Later in the day No 401 Sqn Spitfires attacked the airfield at Hagenow, catching a dozen Fw 190Ds from I./JG 26 as they were forming up for a mission to Lüneburg. Sqn Ldr W T Klersy (in PL344) dove into the midst of the formation, shooting down a fighter for his 11th victory. The Germans claimed two Spitfires shot down, although none were as much as damaged.

It had been a good day for the wing, with seven enemy aircraft destroyed and three damaged. The score might have been even higher had it not been for a shortage of aircraft due to ongoing fuel and ammunition woes.

20 April would also prove bountiful for the pilots of No 126 Wing, and No 401 Sqn in particular, but not before two Spitfires had been lost in separate incidents. No 411 Sqn's Flg Off F R Dennison (in MJ334) escaped unscathed when his engine failed on take-off at 1045 hrs. Twenty minutes later WO V E Barber (in RM875) of No 402 Sqn was hit either by flak or debris when strafing a train near Kiel. He bailed out and evaded, returning to the unit on 3 May.

At 1600 hrs No 401 Sqn pilots spotted a number of fighters taking off from a grass strip southwest of Schwerin, with others patrolling above them. Attacking at once, the unit claimed no fewer than 11 Bf 109s shot down and three more damaged, for the loss of Flg Off R W Anderson (in MJ980), who was shot down and killed by the airfield defences while pursuing a Bf 109 over the strip. Sqn Ldr W T Klersy (in PL344) claimed one and one shared with Flt Lt L W Woods (in ML141), who also downed a fighter by himself. Flg Off J A Ballantine (in MH479) and Flt Lt W R Tew (in MH456) claimed two apiece, these victories taking the latter pilot's final wartime tally to four destroyed and three damaged. Finally, single kills were credited to Flt Lts R H Cull (in MJ340) and J MacKay (in MJ794) and Flg Offs J H Ashton (in NH152) and J P W Francis (in PL402).

No 401 Sqn's Flt Lt B B Mossing was badly injured at 1900 hrs when he was forced to crash-land his Spitfire (MK392, which had been Wg Cdr 'Johnnie' Johnson's JEJ for much of 1944, claiming 13 victories with it) near B116. The fighter's engine cut out on take-off, resulting in a hard impact that ripped its wings off and ended with the aircraft bursting into flames. Mossing extricated himself from the wreckage, despite suffering from a broken leg. Accidents like this routinely occurred within No 126 Wing, and some of the mishaps were blamed on the introduction of 150-grade fuel in early February. The majority of pilots mistrusted the new fuel, and they were relieved when the powers that be reverted back to the 130-grade.

At 1940 hrs a mixed force of 14 aircraft from Nos 401 and 402 Sqns spotted a large number of Luftwaffe fighters taking off from Hagenow. Again the Canadians pulled off a successful 'bounce', claiming seven Fw 190Ds destroyed and three more damaged. Remarkably, Sqn Ldr Klersy (in PL344) would add two more kills to his total for the day, taking his final wartime tally to 14.5 victories and three damaged. Flt Lt Cull (in MK791) and Flg Off Francis (in PL402) would also add single victories to their tallies from earlier in the day, taking their final wartime scores to four destroyed and three damaged each. The final kills went to Flg Offs D B Dack (in NH152) and F D A T Cameron (in MJ794) and Flt Lt L N Watt (in MK203), who were credited with one apiece. Cameron's kill gave him ace status.

Tasked with providing top cover for No 401 Sqn, the pilots of No 402 Sqn were unable to enter the fray in earnest, although Flt Lt R J Taggart (in RM752) and Flg Off T B Lee (in RM651) managed to shoot down an Fw 190D each.

Aside from the 20 aerial victories credited to the wing on this day, its pilots also claimed 34 vehicles destroyed as the Wehrmacht attempted to retreat en masse, despite there being very little room left to withdraw into. The Soviet Red Army was advancing on Berlin in the east and the Anglo-American armies were swiftly moving towards the Elbe River in the south and west.

The 20 kills on 20 April pushed No 126 Wing's tally of aerial victories up to 317 aircraft destroyed since D-Day, and a grand total of 346 since the wing's formation on 4 July 1943. Considering the low serviceability rate for the wing in the final weeks

A burnt out Fw 190D-9 that was destroyed on the ground at an airfield in Germany in 1945. Nicknamed the 'Dora', it was Germany's best piston-engined fighter of the war. One of the first units to equip with the Fw 190D-9 was III./JG 54, which had the onerous task of defending the Me 262 airfields at Hesepe and Achmer, near the Dutch border. This unit regularly fought with No 126 Wing in the final months of the conflict (*Public Archives of Canada PA 145786*)

Flg Off Carl Ellement of No 411 Sqn had the misfortune to be shot down twice by flak, landing behind enemy lines on both occasions. Indeed, he was shot down on his very first mission, on 20 January 1945! After making it back to his unit on 3 April, Ellement was brought down again 18 days later. He rejoined No 411 Sqn on 3 May (*Author's Collection via Chris Thomas*)

Shooting down an enemy aircraft was an extremely difficult thing to do, and Flt Lt Art Tooley of No 411 Sqn was one of the many pilots who was never able to achieve this. He did finish the war with two damaged Fw 190s to his credit, however. Here, Tooley discusses a mechanical issue with LAC Ken Allenby in the spring of 1945 (*DND PL 28259*)

of the conflict, these numbers were impressive.

On 21 April only 48 sorties were flown by all four squadrons due to the wing's by now chronic shortage of airworthy Spitfires. Nevertheless, a handful of Bf 109 claims were made, the first of which saw No 402 Sqn's Flt Lt E R Burrows (in RM651) credited with shooting one down at 1600 hrs near Uelzen. Two more were damaged by other pilots from the unit.

At 1810 hrs No 411 Sqn mounted an armed reconnaissance, during which the unit attacked a train. Flg Off C A E Ellement (in PL283) was hit by flak at this point and forced to bail out near Kiel. He evaded capture for a second time (he had also been shot down by flak on 20 January) and returned to the wing on 3 May. A few minutes later Flt Lt S M McClarty (in RR201) spied a lone Bf 109 north of Putlitz and shot it down.

The next day at 1740 hrs Flt Lts M F Doyle (in MK788) and E T Gardner (PV230) of No 411 Sqn shared in the destruction of an Fw 190 near Salzwedel despite ten-tenths cloud virtually reaching the ground. Poor weather would restrict the wing's operation for several days, with the next event of note taking place at 0955 hrs on 25 April when Flt Lt L W Woods (in ML141) was hit by flak while attacking a train near Hamburg. He bailed out and successfully evaded.

It was not until the 26th, when conditions improved, that the wing added to its score with some unusual targets found on the ground. All four squadrons were able to carry out patrols and armed reconnaissance missions, and although road and rail traffic was hard to find, No 402 Sqn managed to spot a number of Heinkel He 115 twin-engined seaplanes moored near Putnitz. Flt Lt B E Innes (in MV30) claimed one destroyed and Flt Lt R H Roberts (in RN119) one damaged. No 402 Sqn returned to Putnitz at 0930 hrs the following day, and this time Sqn Ldr D C Gordon (in MV256) and Flg Off A G Ratcliffe (in NH835) each destroyed an He 115 and Flg Off H R Robertson (in RM933) damaged a third.

Weather continued to plague the wing, allowing only 56 sorties to be flown on 28 April. Nevertheless, No 412 Sqn managed to lose two Spitfires in action. The first to go down was Flt Lt L A Stewart (in MJ795), whose fighter was hit

by flak near Fassberg at 1625 hrs. He bailed out over Allied lines and soon returned to his unit. Then at 1950 hrs during an evening patrol, Flt Lt G M Horter (in MJ504) fired his guns at a factory near Lüneburg, only to have the rounds ricochet up and hit his aircraft. Forced to make a wheels up landing with his belly tank still attached, Horter hit the ground at high speed. The tank exploded, ripping his Spitfire apart. It looked as though Horter had been killed in the crash, but two days later Sqn Ldr Boyd

Flt Lt Arnold Gibb (left) of No 412 Sqn shot down two Fw 190s in the span of ten minutes on 29 April 1945 while flying a patrol over the Elbe bridgehead, while squadronmate Flt Lt D J Dewan (right) had claimed a solitary Fw 190 destroyed over Hagenow airfield ten days earlier. Although dashing young fighter boys, this photograph, taken in March 1945, reveals the more mundane aspects of squadron life – laundry (*Public Archives of Canada PMR 78-283*)

pinpointed the location of the wreckage and despatched the wing's medical officer to see if the pilot had indeed survived. Incredibly, Horter was found alive still strapped into his cockpit. Suffering from exposure and a broken arm, the badly injured pilot was extracted from the wreckage and quickly sent off to hospital.

The Allied advance reached the River Elbe on 29 April, and Montgomery's 21st Army Group made the crossing with relative ease at Lauenberg and subsequently made contact with the Red Army. In support of the river crossing, No 412 Sqn flew six patrols over the Elbe bridgehead. The first of these encountered at least ten Fw 190s over Winsen at 1250 hrs, and three enemy fighters were quickly despatched by Flt Lt R L Hazel (in MH492) and Flg Offs J H MacLean (in PV202) and A T Gibb (in PT553). Ten minutes later two more Fw 190s were seen northwest of Lüneburg, one of which was also shot down by Flg Off Gibb.

The final day of April would prove catastrophic for the remaining Luftwaffe fighter units still in the fight in the defence of Germany. As the eastern and western fronts converged, there was little space left for the Jagdwaffe to operate in without being spotted by fighters of the combined Soviet, American, British and Canadian air forces. No 402 Sqn opened the scoring for the wing at 1130 hrs when it attacked Fw 190s over and around Schwerin Lake. Flt Lt S M Knight (in MV252) led the way with two kills, the second of which was a Ju 188 that he spotted to the east of the main engagement. Single Fw 190s were credited to Flt Lts D R Drummond (in RM858), W O Young (in RM902) and F E W Hanton (in NH905), while Flt Lts R J Taggart (in RM845) destroyed two Fw 190s on the ground and B E Innes (in NH835) flamed one.

No 402 Sqn was at it again at 1525 hrs when Flt Lts S M Knight (in MV252) and E R Burrows (in RM651) spotted a lone Ju 188 flying at 1500 ft east of Lübeck. Both shared in the bomber's destruction. Eight more Ju 188s were spotted on an airfield near Ratzeburg a short while later, and two were duly claimed as damaged after a strafing pass.

In the early evening No 412 Sqn undertook an armed reconnaissance of the Hagenow-Schwerin-Wismer area and engaged German fighters near Lauenberg. Sqn Ldr M D Boyd (in PV234) claimed two Bf 109s to achieve ace status, while Flt Lt D M Pieri (in MK827) downed an Fw 190 to 'make ace' too. He had taken off as a 'spare' for the main formation, but when his services were not required he was on the verge of turning back to base when he spotted the lone Focke-Wulf and shot it down. Flt Lts L A Stewart (in PT553) and R B Barker (ML362) claimed the final two Bf 109s, this victory taking the latter pilot's tally to four kills and two damaged.

No 411 Sqn was also operating in the same area at this time, and at 2000 hrs Flg Off M F Doyle (in MJ425) intercepted a solitary Fw 190 that had just bombed Allied troops in the Lauenburg area. He shot it down in flames. Forty-five minutes later, squadronmate Flt Lt S M McClarty (in RR201) force-landed near Scharesbeck after being hit by flak. He returned to the wing the following day.

Post-war scrutiny of Luftwaffe records revealed that it was quite possible that one of the enemy aircraft claimed by No 412 Sqn on 30 April was in fact a Heinkel He 162, as Ltn Hans Rechenberg of II./JG 1 (the second, and last, unit to convert to the type) was reportedly shot down by Spitfires in the Wismar area. If this is indeed true, it would mean that the wing downed three types of German jet, namely the Me 262, Ar 234 and He 162.

Twelve aerial victories on the last day of April would give No 126 Wing its best month of the entire war. Some Luftwaffe pilots had shown skill when engaged, but the majority had revealed little willingness to fight. This in turn meant that most victories came easily to the pilots involved. Their achievement of 58 aircraft destroyed, one probable and 31 damaged was a remarkable feat, nevertheless. Equally impressive was the number of sorties flown in spite of chronic shortage of supplies that led to poor airworthiness amongst the Spitfires.

Personnel of No 411 Sqn pose for the camera in April 1945 at B88 Heesch. In the back row, from left to right, are Flg Off T E Vance, Plt Off D B Young, Flg Offs J V McCabe, J T Olson, B A McPhail and J L St John, Sqn Ldr J N Newell (sat on the propeller hub), Flg Off M R Macklem, Flt Lt A Ustenov, Flg Offs C D W Wilson and G N Smith, Flt Lt W A Reid and Plt Off J O A Watt. In the front row, from left to right, are Flg Offs H Martensen, T L O'Brien and C A E Ellement, Flt Lts J M McConnell and D J Bazett, Flg Off J A Doran, Flt Lt D C Gordon, Flg Off G R Panchuk (Intelligence Officer), Flt Lts J J Boyle, W T Gill, M F Doyle and A A W Orr and Flg Offs M G Graham, J F Shiriff and W G Pryde (Public Archives of Canada PMR 78-342)

By the spring of 1945 No 126 Wing was being led by nine-victory ace Wg Cdr G W Northcott (*Canadian Forces*)

Wg Cdr G M Northcott's summary for April details the month's activities, and it also gives some interesting insights into the final weeks of the war in Europe;

'With the wing operating further behind the lines for a large part of the month, fewer sorties were flown than in March, but a substantial increase was revealed in the wing's total operational hours for the month. Sorties numbered 2575 in all, and hours 4172, and the latter figure is a record since the formation of the wing. The first two days were the only ones on which no flying was done, so the last full month of ground and air warfare was helped considerably by the weather.

'A total of 391 missions were flown during the month, and these were divided into 279 missions on patrol, 103 missions on armed reconnaissance and nine missions on escort to medium bombers.

'The patrols made up a large percentage of the total missions for the month. This is largely explained by the fact that during the first two weeks of April the wing was still based at B88 Heesch, which was so far behind the actual frontlines that patrols of the frontline itself and the Rhine River bridges were about all that we could accomplish. Following the wing's move forward to B116 Wunstorf in the middle of the month, patrols were limited and Armed Reconnaissance predominated, with a few escort missions. Missions flown from B116 consisted of frontline cover and patrols over the Elbe River.

'No fighter sweeps or dive-bombing missions were flown during the month.

'Armed Reconnaissance was possible after arrival at B116, and these missions were the source of practically all the wing's imposing ground and air score for the month. The total score of enemy aircraft – 58-1-31, which includes 6-0-8 on the ground – represents a big increase over March, and also the last dying effort of the Luftwaffe. During the first two weeks of the month while the Wing was still located at Heesch and flying only defensively, very few enemy aircraft were sighted, and our claims totalled 2-1-6. On moving to Wunstorf, half-a-dozen of the main German airfields that were still operational were brought well within our range, and this explains the large bag in the last two weeks.

'The total enemy aircraft destroyed represented a record month, and enabled the wing to retain its position of having to its credit the most enemy aircraft destroyed in 2nd TAF. The totals as at 30 April were 370-17-162.

'There were three big days during the month – the 19th, 20th and 30th. The wing's scores on these days were 7-0-3, 20-0-6 and 15-0-8, respectively. The highlight of the month was the score amassed by No 401 Sqn on 20 April when it destroyed 18 enemy aircraft and damaged six. This represents a record for No 126 Wing, if not No 83 Group or the 2nd TAF.

'While many more enemy aircraft were sighted and engaged during the last two weeks of the month, it is felt that this did not reflect any determined offensive action on the part of the Luftwaffe, but rather a pinching between the Eastern and Western fronts, resulting in all remaining German airfields coming within our range, and therefore being subject to strafing attacks and bombing. The Allied advance across the Elbe resulted in only sporadic attacks by single or small groups of enemy aircraft on the bridges and on our forward troops. Again this month much credit for the wing's score must go to the Group Control Centre controllers, who did a good job of locating enemy aircraft and vectoring our Spitfires.

'Our location at B88 dictated our tactics for the first two weeks, when practically nothing but patrols were flown. During the last two weeks armed reconnaissance flown in squadron strength well behind the frontlines proved very productive. As the advance across the Elbe expanded, and more and more limitations were imposed on attacking ground targets, armed reconnaissance became more like fighter sweeps, with squadrons only attacking the juiciest targets. Flak along the Elbe River in particular and flak cars on practically all trains sighted toward the end of the month made attacks on these targets rather dangerous. Opposition by German pilots once they were engaged was frequently the toughest experienced by our pilots since D-Day.

'Losses of pilots for the month totalled eight, as against seven for March. However, considering the number of hours flown during the two months, the ratio is the same, and an improvement over both January and February. Furthermore, of the eight not yet returned pilots, four are now back with us. Of the remaining four, one was caused by the blast of a petrol train being attacked, one was shot down and two were hit by enemy flak.

'With only two non-operational flying days, instruction on a wing basis was necessarily curtailed, and was limited to instruction on Russian aircraft and the customary "48-hour familiarisation programme for new pilots". With the fluid battle conditions of the last two weeks of the month, and the resulting limitations on attacks, briefings were longer and more exacting, and post-mission interrogations provided much ground movement information that was passed on quickly to the army.'

Northcott's comments detailing the differences between flying patrols or armed reconnaissance once again revealed the Spitfire's Achilles' heel – its short range. When based at B88, the wing could only fly patrols, and therefore saw little action. It was too far behind the frontlines. But when the wing moved up to B116, its units were again right behind the frontlines, and closer to the fighting. The Spitfire's short range also had other consequences. More landings and take-offs were required to keep aircraft in the air, which increased the chances of accidents and mishaps. When equipped with bombs, the Spitfire's range was further reduced, thus greatly restricting the number of targets the wing could attack.

April 1945 would be the last full month of the war in Europe. It was now only a matter of days before the Germans surrendered, but the pace of operations did not slow down. On 1 May low cloud prevented an all out effort over the wing's assigned tactical area. Patrols were flown but were mainly uneventful, although Sqn Ldr W T Klersy (in PL344) and Wg Cdr G W Northcott (serial unknown) were each credited with an Fw 190 damaged – this was the latter pilot's sole claim during his brief time leading No 126 Wing.

Flak continued to be Germany's most effective form of defence, downing No 401 Sqn ace Flt Lt G D A T Cameron (in MJ854).

Wg Cdr Geoff Northcott was issued with this personally marked Spitfire XIV (MV263/JEFF) in the autumn of 1945 (via C G Jefford)

Despite being badly burned, he bailed out near Schwerin airfield and was captured. Successfully concealing his side arm, Cameron used it to help him escape the next day with a German doctor as a hostage!

No 411 Sqn's Plt Off P B Young (in TA839) was not so fortunate, as he became disorientated in cloud during an armed reconnaissance north of Hagenow and crashed to his death.

2 May saw No 126 Wing flying standing patrols despite the 'duff weather'. The highlight of the day was when AOC-in-C of the 2nd TAF, AM Sir Arthur Coningham, landed at B116. There, he was presented with a captured Mercedes staff car! Even with the bad weather, the patrols did produce some useful results. Flying between Ahrensburg and Zarrentin at 1130 hrs, Flg Offs C D W Wilson (in ML396) and G N Smith (in MK788) intercepted two tactical reconnaissance Bf 109s from 1./NAGr 3 near Lübeck. Wilson shot one of them down, while Smith damaged an Me 262 a few minutes later.

The next day would bring the last large scale victories for the wing, and also the final casualties. Things did not start well when veteran No 411 Sqn pilot Flt Lt Stan McClarty (in NH263) was wounded in the leg by flak near Kiel at 0805 hrs. While being escorted home he lost consciousness and crashed to his death. McClarty had been one of the 'old timers' of the wing, and his loss was keenly felt with it happening so close to the end of he war.

At 1040 hrs a section of No 402 Sqn fighters led by Sqn Ldr D C Gordon (in RM933) found several Fi 156 Storchs on the ground north of Neumunster and duly strafed them. Minutes later Gordon spotted a single Fi 156 flying at treetop height near Husum airfield, and he quickly shot it down – this took his final tally to nine and two shared destroyed, five probables and five damaged.

No 126 Wing suffered its final combat fatality of the war at 1135 hrs when the fighter of American ace Flt Lt Don Pieri (in MK827) was hit by ricocheting bullets fired from his own cannons while strafing. Although seen to bail out, the No 412 Sqn pilot did not become a PoW and his body was never found.

At 1340 hrs Sqn Ldr W T Klersy (in PL433) and the rest of No 401 Sqn discovered 25+ barely camouflaged aircraft parked on a grass airfield east of Kiel. They were a mix of mostly Ju 52/3m transports and a few He 111s. The strafing attacks were a success, with a dozen Junkers transports being destroyed along with two He 111s and one Ju 87. While the numbers were impressive, most if not all of these aircraft had already been abandoned due to a lack of fuel and unserviceability, and they posed no threat to the Allies. Attacking such targets only exposed pilots to deadly German flak for no real value.

Flg Off D B Dack (in PT582) claimed three Ju 52/3ms destroyed, as did Flg Off R C Gudgeon (in MJ340), while Flg Offs J E Cottrell (in MJ283) and J P W Francis (in PL402) got two each. A Junkers transport and an He 111 were destroyed by Sqn Ldr Klersy, while Flt Lt L H Watt (serial unknown) also got a Ju 52/3m and a Ju 87. Finally, Plt Off A K Woodill (in MH432) destroyed an He 111.

4 May would see the last aerial victory scored by No 126 Wing. No 411 Sqn Spitfires took off at 0540 hrs for the first patrol of the day, and Flt Lt D F Campbell (in PV148) and Flg Off T L O'Brien (in MK686) encountered a lone He 111 near Flensberg an hour later. They made short work of the bomber. That afternoon, before the weather closed in, No 402 Sqn flew a sweep over southern Denmark and shot up several ground targets. 'A venturesome Me 262 took objection to this and shot up one of our kites before withdrawing smartly'. The end result of this lone attack was No 402 Sqn's Flt Lt J E Rigby landing at Wunstorf with a scratched nose and wounded pride. It had been a narrow escape, and the last hostile encounter between a No 126 Wing aircraft and a Luftwaffe fighter. That evening all German forces in northwest Germany and northern Holland laid down their arms. All hostilities would cease at 0800 hrs on 5 May.

Appropriately, the last mission flown by No 126 Wing saw the squadron commanders led on a patrol by Wing Leader Wg Cdr Geoff Northcott. Over the next few days uneventful patrols were flown, and VE-Day was officially marked on 8 May. Sqn Ldr Don Laubman and Flt Lt Jake Maurice also returned to the wing on the 8th looking no worse for wear, having both been shot down in April.

The war in Europe was over. The constant state of readiness, sharp focus, fear, adrenaline rushes and keen sense of purpose that had became a way of life was now replaced by a routine that was strangely empty of purpose, but tempered by a weary satisfaction and place of pride. Before the German surrender, many of the wing personnel saw the horrors of the Belsen concentration camp. Their response was immediate and direct, with a huge truckload of food and medicine being hastily shipped to the camp.

On 12 May the wing moved to B152 Fassburg in support of the British Army of Occupation. For the next two months the flying became routine. Tours expired and men went home. Sadly, peacetime

This clipped wing version of the remarkable Spitfire XIV belonged to No 402 Sqn, and it was photographed at Wunstorf airfield in late May 1945. The clipped wings improved the aircraft's rate of roll at lower altitudes. This version also featured a bubble canopy and was armed with two 20 mm cannon and two 0.50-in machine guns (*Canadian Warplane Heritage Museum*)

flying could, and did, claim lives. On 22 May No 401 Sqn's CO, and high-scoring ace, Sqn Ldr Bill Klersy was killed after his aircraft slammed into a hill in thick cloud during a training exercise. He was just 23 years old. In July the wing moved again, this time to B174 Utersen, northwest of Hamburg, where it became part of the British Air Force of Occupation (BAFO). As 2nd TAF reorganised, so Nos 401 and 402 Sqns were disbanded, leaving Nos 411 and 412 Sqns at B174. No 126 Wing would serve with the BAFO until 1 April 1946, when it was finally disbanded.

No 126 Wing's contribution to the victory in Europe was considerable. It was the highest scoring wing in the 2nd TAF with 333 enemy aircraft destroyed since D-Day, and of the 26 pilots in the 2nd TAF who shot down six or more enemy aircraft, 11 of them were from No 126 Wing.

A summary from No 83 Group, dated 4 May 1945, provides some key insights into the efforts made by the entire group during April;

'A month with no blank days, although weather seriously curtailed operations on several days. It will always be remembered as the month of the chase over Germany, a month in which successes were great, in spite of supply difficulties, and targets were plentiful. However, ammunition was in short supply, and this meant that some enemy got away – this fact was indeed painful to bear.

'The enemy has not carried out a scorched earth policy on his aerodromes. Here and there a determined commander has done his best, but generally booty has been great. The Hun had so many aircraft that he could not move – almost certainly due to petrol shortages and minor unserviceability – that it is not surprising that so many of them should have been destroyed or damaged on the

A rare photograph of Spitfire XIVs of No 411 Sqn at B152 Fassberg in June 1945. This unit re-equipped with the Mk XIV at the end of the war, and it would serve in No 126 Wing as part of the BAFO until finally disbanding at Utersen on 1 April 1946 (Public Archives of Canada PMR 78-52)

Plt Off Eric Slater of No 402 Sqn poses on the wing of a damaged Bf 109 at Wunstorf in May 1945. Its bent propellers indicate that this aircraft must have suffered a recent forced landing. The Bf 109 was the most numerous single-seat fighter employed by the Luftwaffe during the war, but by 9 April 1945 the total number of serviceable examples on strength in the West was just 163 (Canadian Warplane Heritage Museum)

After the war hundreds of German aircraft were found intact. This is an Fw 190F, the ground attack version of the Focke-Wulf fighter. It was extensively modified for the ground attack role through the addition of armour along the underside and sides of the cockpit. Allied fighter-bombers, in contrast, were not modified in any way (apart from bomb racks and rocket rails) for their new role, and suffered as a result. This aircraft was also found at Wunstorf and photographed by Plt Off Eric Slater of No 402 Sqn (*Canadian Warplane Heritage Museum*)

Plt Off Slater is seen here sitting on what looks to be another Fw 190F. The aircraft's rugged air-cooled BMW 801 engine gave added protection to the pilot, and it could take heavy damage and continue to run, unlike the Spitfire's liquid-cooled Merlin, which could be put out of action very easily (*Canadian Warplane Heritage Museum*)

ground during the month. Claims were air (179-10-58) and ground (56-0-90).

'In the air the Luftwaffe was swamped and appeared to be ineffective, but the early phase of the Elbe crossing could have been made very tricky had the Luftwaffe had more success. Indeed, the effort it attempted to make there in opposition to the crossing was indeed greater than that made over the Rhine bridgehead of Rees-Wesel. Luftwaffe loyalties have always been greater than Wehrmacht loyalties, and the Luftwaffe has shown its desire to work and fight. Although often the standard achieved has been low, on other occasions it was quite obvious that experienced pilots were engaged.

'On the ground, continued retreat, in some cases so hurried as to risk air attack without cover, has produced a welter of targets. The slaughter of mechanised enemy transport (MET) has been greater that at any time in the whole campaign, except perhaps for the short phase of the "Falaise Gap".

'It is possible that April will be the last complete month of the campaign. Should this be the case then the group has finished on a very high note. It will be left to military historians to assess the part played by air power in this campaign, but we know it has been great, and we take not a little pride in our achievements.

'Additions to claims and news of returned pilots comes in almost hourly, but at the time of writing, the figures below represent both the effort and results for No 83 Group for the month and the total from D-Day to 30 April 1945.'

April
Sorties – 14,119
Tanks – 15 destroyed, 25 damaged
MET – 1925 destroyed, 3799 damaged
Locos – 56 destroyed, 457 damaged
Rail Trucks – 492 destroyed, 1726 damaged
Ships – 23 damaged
Barges – 5 destroyed, 143 damaged
Enemy Aircraft – 235-10-148

Totals D-Day to 30 April 1945
Sorties – 125,359
Tanks – 389 destroyed, 580 damaged
MET – 8393 destroyed, 15,090 damaged
Locos – 709 destroyed, 2452 damaged
Rail Trucks – 3764 destroyed, 9748 damaged
Ships – 26 sunk, 121 damaged
Barges – 287 destroyed, 121 damaged
Enemy Aircraft – 1133.5-73-656

APPENDICES

KEY DATES

– Formed as No 126 Airfield HQ at RAF Redhill, Surrey, on 4 July 1943
– Redesignated No 126 (Fighter) Wing at RAF Tangmere, Sussex, on 15 May 1944
– Transferred to British Air Forces of Occupation (Germany) on 5 July 1945
– Disbanded at Utersen, Germany, on 1 April 1946

HIGH-SCORING PILOTS WITH No 126 WING

Rank/Name	Total	Squadron/s
Sqn Ldr D C Laubman	15-0-3	412
Sqn Ldr W T Klersy	14.5-0-3	401
Flt Lt J Mackay	11-0-3	401*
Flt Lt R J Audet	10.5-0-1	411
Flt Lt W J Banks	9-3-1	412
Sqn Ldr H C Trainor	8.5-1-0	411 & 401
Flg Off D R C Jamieson	8-0-1	412
Flt Lt G W Johnson	8-0-4	411 & 401
Sqn Ldr R I A Smith	7.2-0-0	401**
Sqn Ldr D C Gordon	7-0-0	442, 411 & 402***
Sqn Ldr L M Cameron	6-0-2	402 & 401
Flt Lt D M Pieri	6-0-2	442 & 412
Flt Lt J J Boyle	5.5-0-1	411
Sqn Ldr R K Hayward	5.5-0.5-5.5	401 & 411
Flt Lt G D A T Cameron	5-1-3	402 & 401
Flt Lt P M Charron	5-0-1	412****
Flg Off M G Graham	5-0-0	411
Flt Lt R R Bouskill	5-0-5	401
Sqn Ldr J E Sheppard	5-0-0	401 & 412
Flt Lt E G Lapp	5-0-1	411
Flt Lt F T Murray	5-1-2.5	412 & 401
Flt Lt R M Davenport	4.5-0-1	401
Sqn Ldr M D Boyd	4.5-0-2	412
Sqn Ldr G D Robertson	4.5-0-1	411*****

Notes

*J MacKay claimed a MiG-15 kill with the USAF on 30/6/53

** R I A Smith would end the war with a total of 13.5-1-1, having claimed 6-1-1 with No 126 Sqn in 1942

*** D C Gordon would end the war with a total of 10-5-5, having claimed 4-5-5 with Nos 274 and 601 Sqns in 1942-43

**** P M Charron ended the war with a total of 7-0-2, having claimed 2-0-1 with No 126 Sqn in 1942

***** G D Robertson ended the war with a total of 4.5-1-4.5, having claimed 0-1-3.5 with Nos 402 and 421 Sqns in 1941-42

SQUADRON SCORES/STATISTICS

Prior to D-Day, No 126 Wing consisted of Nos 401, 411 and 412 Sqns. Their combined score was 29 enemy aircraft destroyed before D-Day. No 442 Sqn joined the wing in July 1944 and left in March 1945, while No 402 Sqn joined the wing in December 1944. Between D-Day and VE-Day, the units achieved the following scores;

No 401 Sqn – 112 enemy aircraft destroyed

No 412 Sqn – 92 enemy aircraft destroyed

No 411 Sqn – 75 enemy aircraft destroyed

No 442 Sqn – 36 enemy aircraft destroyed

No 402 Sqn – 18 enemy aircraft destroyed

No 126 Wing's total score from D-Day to VE-Day was 333 enemy aircraft destroyed. From July 1943 to VE-Day the wing destroyed 362 enemy aircraft and one V1 flying bomb

German Jet Claims

Four Me 262s shot down, 14 damaged, 1 destroyed on the ground

Four Ar 234s shot down, 8 damaged, 3 damaged on the ground

Other totals

4468 enemy vehicles claimed as destroyed or damaged

493 locomotives blown up or disabled

1569 rail trucks in flames or holed

426 rail cuts

Ammunition Consumed

3,421,527 rounds of 20 mm, 0.50-in and 0.303-in

4426 500-lb bombs

3883 250-lb bombs

Sorties flown

22,373

Losses from D-Day to VE-Day

131 Spitfires

98 Pilots

Commanders

Wg Cdr J E Walker – 9 July 1943 to 26 August 1943

Wg Cdr K L B Hodson – 27 August 1943 to 19 July 1944

Grp Capt G R McGregor – 20 July 1944 to 1 April 1946

Wing Commanders Flying

Wg Cdr B D Russel – 9 July 1943 to 16 October 1943

Wg Cdr R W McNair – 17 October 1943 to 12 April 1944

Wg Cdr G C Keefer – 17 April 1944 to 7 July 1944

Wg Cdr B D Russel – 8 July 1944 to 26 January 1945

Wg Cdr G W Northcott – 27 January 1945 to 1 April 1946

1

**Spitfire IXB MJ255/VZ-S of Flt Lt H G Garwood,
No 412 Sqn, Tangmere, 11 June 1944**
On 11 June 1944 Flt Lt H G Garwood's Spitfire MJ255
suffered engine failure whilst patrolling over the D-Day
beachhead at 1350 hrs, although he managed to force land
the aircraft in Allied territory near Tilly-sur-Suelles. A day
later he was back on duty, but his mount (which had
served with No 412 Sqn since November 1943) was listed
as 'category E' written off, salvage impossible.

2

**Spitfire IXB NH260/YO-W of Flt Lt I F Kennedy,
No 401 Sqn, B4 Bény-sur-Mer, France, 28 June 1944**
'Hap' Kennedy was already an ace when he joined No 401
Sqn on 15 June, and he claimed his final two kills with
the unit shortly after it had been sent to France post-
invasion. The first of these came in this aircraft during the
evening of 28 June when an armed reconnaissance by
No 401 Sqn was 'bounced' by a dozen Fw 190s and a large
dogfight ensued. The unit claimed four destroyed, with
one being credited to Kennedy. This was NH260's second
Focke-Wulf of the day, as Flt Lt R M Stayner had downed
one at 0910 hrs. The latter was at its controls again the
following day when he destroyed a Bf 109 over the
Argentan-Falaise area. Stayner claimed his third, and last,
victory (another Fw 190) in NH260 on 20 July, this kill
taking No 401 Sqn's overall tally to exactly 100. Seven
days later Flt Lt A F Halcrow downed a Bf 109 while flying
this aircraft southwest of Caen. On the last day of July
Sqn Ldr H C Trainor claimed his eighth, and last, kill in
NH260 when he despatched an Fw 190 east of Domfront.
Fellow ace Flt Lt R R Bouskill was piloting this aircraft on
17 August when he downed yet another Fw 190 for his
third of five victories. The following day, however, Sqn Ldr
Trainor was forced to crash-land NH260 behind enemy
lines after it was hit by flak near Lisieux. The aircraft had
spent its short frontline career flying exclusively with
No 401 Sqn.

3

**Spitfire IXB MJ202/YO-A of Flg Off A L Sinclair,
No 401 Sqn, B68 Le Culot, Belgium, late September 1944**
Flt Lt Sinclair was one of five pilots to be credited with a
share in the Me 262 downed by No 401 Sqn on 5 October,
although he was flying MK698 at the time – this claim took
his final score to two and two shared destroyed and two
damaged. His mount prior to this was MJ202, which joined
No 401 Sqn on 14 September. The aircraft survived the
war and was eventually scrapped in January 1951.

4

**Spitfire IXE MJ520/Y2-R of Sqn Ldr W A Olmsted,
No 442 Sqn, B68 Le Culot, Belgium, 29 September 1944**
On 20 July 1944, then Flt Lt Olmsted claimed two Fw 190s
destroyed near St Lô in this machine, which was
damaged by debris from one of his victims. Exactly a
week later No 442 Sqn was bounced by 40 Fw 190s and
Bf 109s over Dreux, in Normandy, and one of the attackers
was claimed as a probable by W A Olmsted, who was
again flying this aircraft. This was his last success in the
air, Olmsted's tally finishing on three destroyed, two

probables and three damaged. He became CO of No 442
Sqn in September, and on 14 December was shot down
while strafing a train. Olmsted managed to glide his
aircraft back over the Rhine to friendly territory, where he
bailed out. Canadian troops drove him back to base.
MJ520 was issued new to No 132 Sqn June 1944, before
joining No 442 Sqn the following month. Post-war it was
transferred to the *Armée de l'Air* in September 1946 and
saw service in French Indochina.

5

**Spitfire IXB MK577/YO-F of Sqn Ldr R I A Smith,
No 401 Sqn, B84 Rips, Holland, 5 October 1944**
Malta ace Rod Smith claimed 7.2 victories in the latter half
of 1944 while flying with No 401 Sqn. His last victory – a
one-fifth share in the first Me 262 to be shot down by
the Allies – came in MK577 on 5 October. Six days earlier
Flg Off J C Hughes had claimed a brace of Bf 109s
destroyed with it during the defence of Nijmegen.
Delivered new to No 329 Sqn in June 1944, MK577 was
then handed over to No 411 Sqn in late August. The
fighter was transferred to No 401 Sqn just days later, and
it eventually wound up with the Belgian Air Force in July
1948.

6

**Spitfire IXB ML269/YO-D of Flt Lt R M Davenport,
No 401 Sqn, B84 Rips, Holland, 5 October 1944**
ML269 was also involved in the historic Me 262
engagement on 5 October 1944, being flown by Flt Lt
Davenport at the time. His combat report from this mission
read as follows – 'I was flying as "Yellow 1" in No 401
"Blackout" Sqn when we sighted an Me 262 at 12,000 ft,
five miles northeast of Nijmegen. There was a great mix-
up as all 12 Spits dove for the jet job. I waited until he
made his first break, then came in at 20 degrees line astern
at approximately 450 mph. I gave a three-second burst at
400 yards and observed strikes on the fuselage. I then
continued the chase, which was composed of rolls, dives
and turns at approximately 375 mph. I finally closed in to
300 yards line astern and emptied the remainder of my
guns – approximately ten to twelve seconds worth – into
the kite, observing strikes all over its engines and fuselage.
The aircraft was burning all this time. The pilot appeared
to be unhurt, and he put up a good fight throughout the
engagement before at last realising that the fight was up.
He attempted to turn away from "Red 1" as he lost height,
then crashed and burned. I used camera and got eight feet
of film, showing both cannon and machine gun strikes.
My gyro gunsight functioned properly, and I landed with
no ammunition left. I claim one-fifth of an Me 262
destroyed'. Initially issued to No 441 Sqn in July 1944, this
aircraft joined No 401 Sqn late the following month.
Surviving the war, it was transferred to the Royal Hellenic
Air Force in July 1947

7

**Spitfire IXB MJ852/YO-S of Flt Lt H J Everard, No 401 Sqn,
B84 Rips, Holland, 5 October 1944**
Future No 401 Sqn CO, and ace, Flt Lt Everard was also
awarded a one-fifth share in the Me 262 destroyed on 5
October 1944 while flying MJ852. Delivered new to No 411

Sqn on 14 September 1944, the fighter was used by Flt Lt J M McConnell to claim an Fw 190 destroyed 13 days later. The Spitfire was then passed on to No 401 Sqn, and MJ852 remained with the unit until Christmas Day 1944, when now Sqn Ldr Everard was forced to bail out of it south of Venlo when the fighter was hit by debris from a Bf 109 that was being attacked by another pilot.

8
Spitfire IXB MJ726/YO-Z of Flt Lt J MacKay, No 401 Sqn, B84 Rips, Holland, 5 October 1944
Future ace Flt Lt MacKay also got a one-fifth share in the Me 262 kill on 5 October 1944 while flying MJ276. This was the first of his 11 and 2 shared victories, and the only one he claimed in this aircraft. There is some confusion as to which Spitfire MacKay was flying when he attacked the Me 262, as according to squadron records MJ726 was shot down by an Fw 190 three days earlier whilst being flown by WO W M Thomas! However, this serial has also been assigned to MacKay for his Me 262 success. The aircraft was delivered new to No 312 Sqn in February 1944, transferred to No 442 Sqn on 24 August and then handed over to No 401 Sqn one week later.

9
Spitfire IXE MK686/DB-R of Flt Lt J J Boyle, No 411 Sqn, B88 Heesch, Holland, December 1944 to February 1945
Flt Lt Boyle named this Spitfire Sweet Sue V after his newborn daughter. One of No 411 Sqn's aces with 5.5 victories to his name, Boyle claimed an Me 262 shot down while flying this aircraft on Christmas Day 1944. MK686 was also used by Flg Off D J Bazett to down an Fw 190 (part of a 'Mistel' composite aircraft) on 16 April 1945 and by Flg Off T L O'Brien to share in the destruction of an He 111 on 4 May. The latter was the last aerial victory to fall to No 126 Wing. Initially delivered to No 66 Sqn in June 1944, MK686 joined No 411 Sqn six months later. It was briefly loaned to No 414 Sqn in April 1945, but had been returned to No 411 Sqn by month-end. Post-war, MK686 was transferred to the Armée de l'Air on 31 July 1946.

10
Spitfire IXE RR201/DB-G of Flt Lt R J Audet, No 411 Sqn, B88 Heesch, Holland, 29 December 1944
Flt Lt Audet was one of the few Allied pilots to become an 'ace in a day' during World War 2 – a feat he achieved in the space of just ten minutes, despite having never seen an enemy aircraft before. On 29 December 1944 he shot down three Fw 190s and two Bf 109s in this very aircraft. Audet also used it to destroy an Fw 190 on 14 January and an Me 262 nine days later. Delivered new to No 66 Sqn in October 1944, RR201 was subsequently transferred to No 411 Sqn. Aside from Audet, two other pilots in his unit also claimed kills with the fighter, Flg Off C D W Wilson downing an He 111 on 20 April 1945 and Flt Lt S M McClarty destroying a Bf 109 the following day. RR201 was being flown by the latter when it was written off on 30 April after McClarty force-landed near Scharesbeck with a flak-damaged engine.

11
Spitfire IXE MJ445/YO-A of Flg Off G D A T Cameron, No 401 Sqn, B88 Heesch, Holland, 1 January 1945

No 401 Sqn ace Flg Off Cameron claimed three of his five aerial kills in this aircraft on the morning of 1 January 1945 when No 126 Wing opposed the Luftwaffe's daring Operation Bodenplatte. No 401 Sqn was preparing to take-off on a patrol when 40+ Bf 109s and Fw 190s swept over B88 en route to other airfield targets. Its Spitfires scrambled immediately, and in the next ten minutes Flg Off Cameron shot down three Bf 109s.

12
Spitfire IXE MK686/DB-L of Flt Lt J J Boyle, No 411 Sqn, B88 Heesch, Holland, early January 1945
On Christmas Day 1944 Flt Lt Boyle returned to base early in this aircraft when his wingman's Spitfire started to run roughly. In an effort to rid himself of excess height as he approached B88, Boyle stuck the fighter's nose down in a spiral dive and shot past 500 mph. At this point he spotted a single Me 262 from II./KG 51 over the airfield, and with his high speed he quickly got onto its tail. Boyle opened fire and hit the Me 262 several times before it crashed at a flat angle and burst into flames. This was Boyle's second aerial victory. Four days later Flg Off R A Gilberstad claimed an Fw 190 that spun into the ground whilst in pursuit of MK686. Delivered to No 66 Sqn in June 1944, this aircraft joined No 411 Sqn just four days before Boyle claimed his Me 262. Passed on to No 414 Sqn in April 1945, it was eventually struck off charge in July 1946.

13
Spitfire IXB MJ980/YO-M of Flt Lt J MacKay, No 401 Sqn, B88 Heesch, Holland, 14 January 1945
Flt Lt MacKay used MJ980 to destroy three Fw 190s from I./JG 1 in a single sortie over Twente airfield on 14 January 1945, thus 'making ace'. He had also downed a Bf 109 in this machine on Christmas Day 1944. Finally, Flt Lt M Thomas was flying MJ980 when he shared in the destruction of an 'Me 262' (probably an Ar 234) on 23 January. Initially issued to No 421 Sqn in January 1944, the aircraft joined No 403 Sqn four months later and was eventually transferred to No 401 Sqn in December of that year. It was lost on 20 April 1945 when Flg Off R W Anderson was shot down and killed by airfield defences south of Schwerin while pursuing a Bf 109.

14
Spitfire IXE PT883/Y2-A of Flt Lt J E Reade, No 442 Sqn, B88 Heesch, Holland, 14 January 1945
Delivered new to No 127 Sqn in late November 1944, this aircraft joined No 442 Sqn in mid-December as an attrition replacement. On the 27th of that month Flg Off M A Perkins damaged an Me 262 with it near Aachen, and on 14 January Flt Lt J E Reade used PT883 to destroy an Fw 190 over Twente airfield. A brace of Bf 109s fell to the Spitfire's guns on 25 February when Plt Off E C Baker downed two west of Rheine. Having survived the war, PT883 was eventually sold to the Turkish air force in August 1947.

15
Spitfire IXB ML141/YO-E of Flg Off D F Church, No 401 Sqn, B88 Heesch, Holland, 23 January 1945
Flg Off Church served with No 401 Sqn between 4 August 1944 and 19 April 1945, claiming three aircraft destroyed

and two damaged during his tour. The last of his kills came in this aircraft on 23 January 1945 when he downed an Ar 234 that had just taken off from Bramsche airfield, north of Osnabrück. Three weeks earlier, ML141 had also been used by Flt Lt J C Lee to down a Bf 109 on 1 January. And on 20 April Flt Lt L W Woods claimed one and one shared Bf 109s destroyed with the fighter. Five days later Woods was forced to abandon ML141 near Hamburg after it was hit by flak during a strafing attack on a train. Initially delivered to No 414 Sqn in late August 1944, the fighter had joined No 401 Sqn on 21 December.

16
Spitfire IXB MK791/YO-Y of Flt Lt W C Connell, No 401 Sqn, B88 Heesch, Holland, 23 January 1945
'Bud' Connell claimed three shared victories in this aircraft, being credited with a half-share in an Fw 190 on 21 November 1944, a half-share in a Bf 109 on Christmas Day 1944 and a half-share in an Ar 234 on 23 January 1945. A highly experienced pilot, he had served with No 32 Sqn and No 1 Sqn RCAF in the autumn of 1940, and seen action in the defence of Malta with Nos 126 and 249 Sqns (claiming one destroyed, one probable and three damaged with the latter unit) in 1942. Wounded by the gunner of a Ju 87 on 8 May 1942, Connell was evacuated back to Canada. Fully recovered, he joined No 401 Sqn in May 1944 and served with the unit until April 1945. MK791 was also credited with an Fw 190D destroyed on 20 April 1945, its pilot on this occasion being Flt Lt R H Cull. Delivered new to No 401 Sqn in late September 1944, this aircraft was eventually transferred to No 411 Sqn in late May 1945. Placed in storage post-war, MK791 was overhauled by Westland in 1946 and sold to the *Armée de l'Air* in September of that year.

17
Spitfire XIV RM862/AE-K of Flt Lt K S Sleep, No 402 Sqn, B88 Heesch, Holland, 25 February 1945
Flt Lt Sleep saw considerable action in this aircraft on 25 February 1945, as the following excerpt from No 126 Wing's Summary of Operations No 240 reveals – 'The No 402 Sqn commitment for today was dive-bombing the railway from Borken to Emmerich. In sections of six aircraft led by Flt Lts Sleep, Moore and Whittaker, they flew five missions totalling 27 sorties and claimed an Me 262 damaged (shared by Flt Lts Sleep and Innis), three rail cuts, two mechanised transport damaged, one loco destroyed and one damaged and one horse-drawn transport and one flak tower damaged'. Sleep had also claimed No 402 Sqn's first aerial victory of 1945 in this aircraft when he downed a Ju 88 from NJG 2 on 8 February. RM862 had been delivered to No 402 Sqn in early January 1945, and it subsequently joined the Central Fighter Establishment in November 1946. Like a number of other ex-RCAF Spitfire XIVs, it was sold to the Belgian Air Force in August 1947.

18
Spitfire IXB MH847/YO-N of Sqn Ldr W T Klersy, No 401 Sqn, B88 Heesch, Holland, 1 March 1945
Sqn Ldr Klersy downed two Bf 109s and an Fw 190 in this aircraft in the Dorsten area on 1 March 1945 after an armed reconnaissance by Spitfires from both Nos 401 and 412 Sqns was 'bounced' by 40+ enemy fighters. He

had also used this Spitfire to damage an Ar 234 on 23 January. Klersy was the last pilot to fly MH847, for at the end of a mission on 17 April he force-landed the flak-damaged fighter at B116 and the Spitfire subsequently burnt itself out on the grass runway. Issued new to No 317 Sqn in October 1943, it had been transferred to No 332 Sqn in June 1944 and then passed on to No 174 Sqn three months later. MH847 finally joined No 401 Sqn on 4 January 1945.

19
Spitfire IXB MK203/YO-C of Flt Lt L N Watt, No 401 Sqn, B88 Heesch, Holland, 12 March 1945
Flt Lt Watt joined No 401 Sqn in October 1944, and he used this aircraft to down an Me 262 on 12 March and an Fw 190 on 20 April (with a second one damaged on this date). He was also flying MK203 when he destroyed a Ju 87 and Ju 52/3m on the ground at Schonberg on 3 May. MK203 was assigned to No 401 Sqn in November 1944 and passed on to No 130 Sqn in May 1945. Stored for a number of years post-war, it was sold for scrapping in February 1950.

20
Spitfire XIV RM875/AE-H of Flg Off H C Nicholson, No 402 Sqn, B88 Heesch, Holland, 13 March 1945
On 13 March 1945 Flg Off Nicholson shot an Ar 234 down while flying this aircraft on a late afternoon sweep near Gladback, The pilot initially claimed an Me 262 destroyed, but this was later changed to an Arado bomber by 2nd TAF HQ after his gun camera film was examined. WO V E Barber bailed out of RM875 on 20 April when the fighter was hit either by flak or debris during a strafing attack on a train near Kiel. The aircraft had served exclusively with No 402 Sqn since late November 1944.

21
Spitfire XIV RM727/AE-P of Flt Lt H A Cowan, No 402 Sqn, B88 Heesch, Holland, 30 March 1945
On 30 March 1945 Flt Lt Cowan (in this aircraft) managed to bounce a formation of 16 Fw 190Ds from I. and IV./JG 26 and shoot down Fw Hans Eisnberg. No 402 Sqn claimed 18 aircraft destroyed while flying the Griffon-engined Spitfire XIV with No 126 Wing. Delivered new to No 91 Sqn on 31 July 1944, RM727 was transferred to No 402 Sqn in November of that same year and eventually struck off charge and scrapped in July 1946.

22
Spitfire XIV RM804/AE-E of Flg Off R W Lawson, No 402 Sqn, B88 Heesch, Holland, 31 March 1945
Flg Off Lawson claimed his only aerial successes of the war in this aircraft on 31 March 1945 when, during an armed reconnaissance over the front, he spotted two Fw 190Ds south of Oldenburg and promptly shot them down. Lawson's combat report recalled the details of the action – 'I was flying "Yellow 3" in No 402 Sqn on Sweep/Armed Reconnaissance when I saw two aircraft passing under our section heading southwest. I called "Red 1" and half-rolled down after the aircraft. I recognised them to be Fw 190s. I picked out the No 2 and fired a second-and-a-half burst from 150 yards at approximately ten degrees to port and slightly above. I saw strikes and a burst of flame from near the cockpit. He

then half-rolled into a wood and exploded. I closed to within 200 yards of the leading enemy aircraft and gave him a half-second burst, but saw no results. I then closed to 100/150 yards dead line astern and fired a second-and-a-half burst. This time I saw strikes and the drop tank and canopy flew off, followed by a burst of flame. The enemy aircraft then did a slight wing over and exploded in a field'. Delivered to No 402 Sqn in January 1945, RM804 was transferred to No 401 Sqn in May and passed on to No 411 Sqn the following month. It was eventually scrapped in May 1954.

23
Spitfire XIV NH744/AE-Z of Sqn Ldr Donald Laubman, No 402 Sqn, B108 Rheine, Germany, 14 April 1945
Already an ace with 14 and 2 shared kills and 3 damaged to his credit following a tour with No 412 Sqn, Don Laubman rejoined No 126 Wing as the new CO of No 402 Sqn on 7 April 1945. He had only been in the job a week when he was forced to bail out of this brand new aircraft over enemy lines. Spotting a pair of German halftracks in the Rethem area, he had strafed one and was lining up the second when his first target exploded. The subsequent fireball engulfed the low-flying Spitfire XIV, literally cooking its Griffon engine. Climbing to 7000 ft with his engine temperature rapidly rising, Laubman headed for Allied territory. His damaged Spitfire soon burst into flames, however, and he was forced to bail out into captivity. Laubman was subsequently reunited with his unit on 5 May. NH744 had only joined No 402 Sqn on 29 March.

24
Spitfire XIV RN119/AE-J of Flg Off C B MacConnell, No 402 Sqn, B116 Wunstorf, Germany, 19 April 1945
On 19 April 1945, Flg Off MacConnell was credited with a Ju 88 destroyed north of the Schweriner See while flying this aircraft. Delivered to No 402 Sqn in February 1945, RN119 was subsequently passed on to No 412 Sqn in late June 1945. As with a number of No 402 Sqn Mk XIVs, the aircraft was eventually transferred (on 19 June 1948) to the Belgian Air Force.

25
Spitfire IXB PL344/YO-H of Sqn Ldr W T Klersy, No 401 Sqn, B116 Wunstorf, 20 April 1945
Ranking No 401 Sqn ace Sqn Ldr Bill Klersy claimed his final 4.5 victories in this aircraft on 19-20 April 1945. He also used PL344 to destroy a Ju 52/3m and an He 111 on the ground on 3 May. Initially issued to No 602 Sqn in mid-August 1944, the fighter joined No 442 Sqn late the following month. Assigned to No 401 Sqn in early 1945, the Spitfire moved to Norway with No 130 Sqn just after VE-Day and was then flown by No 129 Sqn at RAF Church Fenton until the unit disbanded in September 1946. Having been struck off charge by the RAF three months later, PL344 was eventually sent to the Anthony Fokker Technical School, where it was used to demonstrate undercarriage retraction systems in the 1950s and 60s. Subsequently dismantled, the centre fuselage and parts of the wings were bought by the late Charles Church in 1985 and eventually restored to airworthiness between 1988 and 1991. Acquired by Kermit Weeks in 1992, the Spitfire was sold to fellow American Tom Blair in 2001 following

further restoration by Personal Plane Services. Still owned by Blair in 2010, PL344 is presently resident at IWM Duxford, in Cambridgeshire.

26
Spitfire IXB MH456/YO-Z of Flt Lt W R Tew, No 401 Sqn, B116 Wunstorf, Germany, 20 April 1945
Flt Lt Tew downed two Bf 109s in this aircraft on 20 April 1945, thus taking his final wartime tally to four destroyed and three damaged. No 401 Sqn was credited with 11 destroyed and three damaged for the loss of a single Spitfire on this date, with No 126 Wing's overall tally being 20 confirmed victories. A well travelled Spitfire, MH456 had initially served with No 602 Sqn from October 1943, before joining No 453 Sqn in February of the following year. Assigned to No 442 Sqn in December 1944, it was transferred to No 401 Sqn in March 1945 and then No 130 Sqn two months later. The fighter was struck off charge in July 1946.

27
Spitfire XIV MV252/AE-Q of Flt Lt S M Knight, No 402 Sqn, B116 Wunstorf, Germany, 30 April 1945
Two-tour veteran Flt Lt Stan Knight claimed his only victories on 30 April 1945 in this aircraft when he downed an Fw 190 and shared in the destruction of a Ju 88 during a late morning patrol over Schwerin Lake, followed by a Ju 188 shot down east of Lübeck several hours later. MV252 joined No 402 Sqn on 26 April 1945, and it was transferred to No 412 Sqn at the end of June. Issued to No 2 Sqn in June 1948 following an extended spell in storage, MV252 burst a tyre on take-off when departing the unit's Wahn, Germany, base on 25 November that same year, and the fighter was written off in the subsequent belly landing.

28
Spitfire XIV RM785/T of Sqn Ldr W T Klersy, No 401 Sqn, B116 Wunstorf, Germany, May 1945
Sqn Ldr Klersy was one of the top scoring aces in No 126 Wing during the period from D-Day to the end of hostilities. His unit, No 401 Sqn, transitioned to the Spitfire XIV after the cessation of hostilities, although this particular aircraft was on strength from 19 April. Klersy lost his life in RM785 when he crashed in poor weather during a training exercise on 22 May 1945.

29
Spitfire XIV RM933/AE-T of Sqn Ldr D C Gordon, No 402 Sqn, B116 Wunstorf, Germany, 3 May 1945
No 402 Sqn's ace CO Sqn Ldr Gordon claimed his unit's final aerial success of World War 2 when he used this aircraft to down an Fi 156 Storch in a one-sided clash east of Neumunster on 3 May 1945. Gordon has also scored kills with Nos 442 and 411 Sqns immediately prior to becoming No 402 Sqn's last wartime CO in early April 1945. RM933 was delivered to No 402 Sqn in late February 1945, and following time with the Air Service Training Unit at Hamble post-war, the aircraft was transferred to the Belgian Air Force in September 1948.

30
Spitfire XIV MV263/JEFF of Wg Cdr G W Northcott, No 126 Wing, B174 Utersen, Germany, September 1945

Having previously commanded No 402 Sqn, 8.5-victory ace Wg Cdr Geoff Northcott later led the Spitfire-equipped No 126 Wing during the final months of World War 2, flying his personally marked Spitfire IX JEFF. He returned to Canada during the summer of 1945, but in September he rejoined the wing as its CO in Germany. By this stage its squadrons had largely re-equipped with Spitfire XIVs, and MV263 became Northcott's personal mount, carrying his initials to identify it, as was the privilege of his position. Northcott remained in command until the wing disbanded on 1 April 1946. MV263 was later transferred to the Belgian Air Force, serving with the *Ecole de Chasse* until crashing in July 1950.

Back cover

Spitfire IXB MJ854/YO-A of Flt Lt J MacKay, No 401 Sqn, B116 Wunstorf, Germany, 16 April 1945
Intensive air operations began at 0745 hrs on 16 April 1945, led by a solo attack on Ludwigslust airfield by Flt Lt MacKay in this aircraft. Heavy defensive fire forced him to break off the attack, but not before he had damaged three Ar 234 jet bombers on the ground. MacKay had previously used MJ854 to down an Fw 190 and damage a second Focke-Wulf fighter and a Bf 109 in the Dorsten area on 1 March. He followed this success up with two Bf 109s destroyed in this machine near Münster on the 28th of that same month. These were MacKay's final kills in World War 2. Fellow No 401 Sqn ace Flt Lt G D A T Cameron bailed out of a blazing MJ854 after it was hit by flak near Schwerin airfield on 1 May. This aircraft had initially served with No 442 Sqn prior to it being transferred to No 401 Sqn in January 1945.

Unit Heraldry

No 126 Airfield HQ/Wing had no specific badge during its brief existence, although the majority of the squadrons assigned to it did. However, No 442 Sqn proved to be the exception, as no badge was officially authorised for the unit in World War 2. No 401 Sqn's emblem was the head of a Rocky Mountain sheep, which was chosen because the animal was known for its qualities of great stamina and fighting spirit. It is also indigenous to the Rocky Mountain region of Canada. No 402 Sqn adopted the City of Winnipeg Bear, thus denoting where the unit had originally been formed as No 12 Army Cooperation Squadron in October 1932. The standing grizzly bear totem of the North Pacific Coast Indians holds a prominent place in Indian mythology, and it is believed to have supernatural powers. No 411 Sqn's badge boasts a bear rampant – grizzly bears are fierce fighters, and can be found throughout much of Canada. Finally, No 412 Sqn's badge features a falcon volant. The falcon is indigenous to all parts of Canada. Known for its skill and aggressiveness in dealing with its enemies, it has been used for hunting from an early date in history.

BIBLIOGRAPHY

BERGER, MONTY AND BRIAN JEFFERY STREET, *Invasions Without Tears*, Vintage Books, 1994

BRACKEN, ROBERT, *Spitfire – the Canadians*, The Boston Mills Press, 1995

GREENHOUSE, BRERETON, STEPHEN J HARRIS, WILLIAM C JOHNSTON AND WILLIAM G P RAWLING, *The Crucible of War 1939-1945 – The Official History of the Royal Canadian Air Force Vol III*, University of Toronto Press, 1994

JARRETT, PHILIP ed., *Aircraft of the Second World War*, Putnam Aeronautical Books, 1997

JEFFORD, WG CDR C G, *RAF Squadrons*, Airlife, 2001

MACDONALD, G D, *442 Squadron History – 442 Transport and Rescue Squadron*, Canadian Forces Base Comox, 1987

McCLENAGHAN, JOHN AND DEREK BLATCHFORD, *411 Squadron – 50 Years of History*, 411 Tactical Aviation Squadron, 1992

McKINSTRY, LEO, *Portrait of a Legend – Spitfire*, John Murray Publishers, 2007

MORGAN, ERIC B AND EDWARD SHACKLADY, *Spitfire – The History*, Key Publishing, 1993

MORGAN, HUGH, *Me 262 Stormbird Rising*, Osprey Publishing, 1994

NIJBOER, DONALD, *Graphic War – The Secret Aviation Drawings and Illustrations of World War II*, The Boston Mills Press, 2005

PRICE, DR ALFRED *Osprey Aircraft of the Aces 5 – Late Mark Spitfire Aces 1942-45*, Osprey Publishing, 1995

RAWLINGS, JOHN, *Fighter Squadrons of the RAF and their Aircraft*, Crécy Books, 1993

SAMUEL, KOSTENUK, *RCAF – Squadron Histories and Aircraft, 1924-1968*, Samuel Stevens Hakkert, 1977

SHORES, CHRISTOPHER, *Those Other Eagles*, Grub St, 2004

SHORES, CHRISTOPHER AND CLIVE WILLIAMS, *Aces High*, Grub St, 1994

SHORES, CHRISTOPHER, *Aces High Volume 2*, Grub St, 1999

SHORES, CHRISTOPHER AND CHRIS THOMAS, *2nd Tactical Air Force Force Vols 1, 2, 3 and 4*, Classic Publications, 2004, 2005, 2006 and 2008

SMITH, PETER C, *The History of Dive-Bombing*. The Nautical & Aviation Publishing Company, 1981

THOMAS, ANDREW, *Osprey Aircraft of the Aces 81 – Griffon Spitfire Aces*, Osprey Publishing, 2008